MIXON STENHAMN

Mental Toughness for Teen Athletes

Navigate Pressure, Build Focus, Resilience, and Confidence to get an Unstoppable Mindset in 30 Days for Unprecedented Success in Sports and Life

First published by Stoneport & Co AB 2024

Copyright © 2024 by Mixon Stenhamn

All rights reserved. No part of this publication may be reproduced, stored or transmitted in any form or by any means, electronic, mechanical, photocopying, recording, scanning, or otherwise without written permission from the publisher. It is illegal to copy this book, post it to a website, or distribute it by any other means without permission.

Mixon Stenhamn asserts the moral right to be identified as the author of this work.

Mixon Stenhamn has no responsibility for the persistence or accuracy of URLs for external or third-party Internet Websites referred to in this publication and does not guarantee that any content on such Websites is, or will remain, accurate or appropriate.

Designations used by companies to distinguish their products are often claimed as trademarks. All brand names and product names used in this book and on its cover are trade names, service marks, trademarks and registered trademarks of their respective owners. The publishers and the book are not associated with any product or vendor mentioned in this book. None of the companies referenced within the book have endorsed the book.

First edition

This book was professionally typeset on Reedsy.
Find out more at reedsy.com

Contents

Introduction: The Game Plan   vi
  Welcome Note: Get Ready to Win   vi
  Why This Book? Your Roadmap to Success   vi
  How to Use This Book: Your 30-Day Challenge   vii
  Setting the Stage: What to Expect   vii

I Part 1: Preparing the Ground - Mindset Fundamentals

Chapter 1: The Power of Mindset   3
  1.1 Understanding Mindset: Fixed vs. Growth   3
  1.2 Real-Life Examples: Athletes Who Transformed Their Game   5
Chapter 2: The Confidence Code   8
  2.1 Building Unshakeable Confidence   8
  2.2 Overcoming Self-Doubt: Techniques and Strategies   10
Chapter 3: Focus and Concentration   14
  3.1 Developing Laser-Sharp Focus   14
  3.2 Techniques to Eliminate Distractions   17

II Part 2: Daily Drills – Your 30-Day Action Plan

Week 1: Setting the Foundation   25
  Day 1: Goal Setting and Visualization   25
  Day 2: Positive Affirmations   27
  Day 3: Understand Your Strengths and Weaknesses   30
  Day 4: Develop a Routine   33
  Day 5: The Importance of Sleep and Recovery   35

Day 6: Nutrition and Hydration for Optimal Performance ... 38
Day 7: Rest and Reflection ... 40
Week 2: Building Momentum ... 44
Day 8: Overcoming Fear and Anxiety ... 44
Day 9: Staying Motivated and Avoiding Burnout ... 46
Day 10: The Role of a Positive Attitude ... 49
Day 11: Visualization Techniques ... 51
Advanced Visualization: Beyond the Basics ... 51
Incorporating Visualization into Training ... 52
Real-Life Applications: Stories from the Field ... 53
Day 12: Building Mental Toughness ... 54
Exercises to Develop Mental Toughness ... 54
Role Models: Learning from the Mentally Tough ... 55
Day 13: The Power of Gratitude ... 56
Day 14: Rest and Reflection ... 59
Week 3: Advanced Techniques ... 64
Day 15: Handling Pressure and Expectations ... 64
Day 16: Improving Focus with Meditation ... 66
Day 17: Developing Resilience ... 69
Day 18: The Importance of Teamwork and Communication ... 71
Day 19: Handling Setbacks and Failures ... 74
Day 20: Mental Preparation for Competitions ... 76
Week 4: The Final Push ... 82
Day 22: Integrating Mindfulness into Daily Life ... 82
Day 23: The Role of Mentors and Role Models ... 84
Day 24: Fine-Tuning Your Routine ... 87
Day 25: Reflecting on Your Journey ... 90
Day 26: Maintaining Your Momentum ... 92
Day 27: Setting Future Goals ... 95
Day 28: Visualization and Relaxation ... 98
Day 30: Celebrating Your Achievements ... 100

III   Part 3: Beyond the Finish Line – Sustaining Your Success

Chapter 4: Maintaining Your Unstoppable Mindset	107
4.1 Continuing the Journey: Lifelong Learning	107
4.2 Staying Motivated: Tips and Tricks	109
Chapter 5: Applying Your Skills Beyond Sports	116
5.1 Transferring Your Mindset to Other Areas of Life	116
5.2 Success Stories: From Athletes to Leaders	118
Conclusion: Your New Beginning	122
Appendices	129
Resources for Further Reading	130
Books:	130
Articles and Journals:	131
Websites and Blogs:	131
Podcasts and Videos:	132
Journaling Page for Daily, Weekly & Monthly Reflections	135
Support and Community Resources for Athletes	137
Online Communities	137
Facebook Groups	137
Online Forums	138
Local Organizations and Clubs	138
Professional Support	139
Additional Resources	139
About the Author	141

Introduction: The Game Plan

Welcome Note: Get Ready to Win

Welcome, future champions! You're embarking on a transformative journey designed to unlock your full potential, both on and off the field. Whether you're a seasoned athlete or just starting out, this book is your guide to developing an unstoppable mindset. Picture stepping into every game, practice, or challenge with unshakeable confidence and laser-sharp focus. Sounds pretty great, right? Well, that's precisely what we're aiming for. So, get ready to transform your mental game and prepare to win — because greatness is just 30 days away!

Why This Book? Your Roadmap to Success

Why place your trust in this book as your guide to success? We've distilled the wisdom of top athletes, coaches, and psychologists into a step-by-step program that's not only easy to follow but also proven to work. This isn't just a collection of theories — it's a practical guide designed to produce real, tangible results. Through this book, you'll learn to conquer self-doubt, maintain focus under pressure, and develop the resilience needed to overcome any obstacle. Consider this book your personal coach, arming you with the tools and strategies to achieve greatness in sports and beyond.

How to Use This Book: Your 30-Day Challenge

Here's the game plan: over the next 30 days, you'll engage in daily challenges designed to build your confidence, sharpen your focus, and strengthen your resilience. Each week, we'll focus on different aspects of developing an unstoppable mindset with practical exercises, reflections, and tips to support your growth. You don't need any special equipment — just a commitment to yourself and a willingness to put in the work. Whether you tackle a chapter a day or spread it out over a week, consistency is key. However, my recommendation is that you read only one chapter per day. Achieve every Daily Goal in Part 2 of the Book, and don't forget to reward yourself afterward. Stick with it, and you'll be amazed by your achievements in just one month.

Setting the Stage: What to Expect

Let's break down what you'll explore in this book. It's divided into three parts:

- **Part 1: Preparing the Ground – Mindset Fundamentals**: Here, we lay the foundational skills necessary to build a resilient mindset, enhance confidence, and sharpen focus.
- **Part 2: Daily Drills – Your 30-Day Action Plan**: The core of the book, where you'll find your daily challenges organized week by week, each designed to fortify your mental toughness systematically.
- **Part 3: Beyond the Finish Line – Sustaining Your Success**: In this section, we'll discuss how to sustain your progress and apply these mental strategies beyond sports, ensuring that your new mindset enriches all areas of your life.

By the end of this journey, not only will you have transformed your mental game, but you'll also have acquired skills that will serve you well in every aspect of life. Ready to get started? Let's dive in and make you unstoppable!

I

Part 1: Preparing the Ground - Mindset Fundamentals

Chapter 1: The Power of Mindset

Ever had one of those days when everything just clicked? Your sneakers feel like they're made of springs, the ball seems to obey your thoughts, and the crowd fades into a distant murmur. Now, think about a day when the opposite happens. Your legs feel like they've been swapped with lead pipes, and the ball feels like a greased melon. What's the difference? Sure, physical condition and external conditions play a part, but the secret ingredient often boils down to something less visible but incredibly powerful — your mindset.

Mindset is not just a fancy buzzword your coach tosses around to sound profound. It's a real, impactful tool that can propel you to heights unimaginable or dump you into the pits of performance despair. And the beauty of it? It's all in your control. Let's unpack this invisible game-changer, shall we?

1.1 Understanding Mindset: Fixed vs. Growth

Fixed Mindset: The Unseen Anchor

A fixed mindset can sneak up on you like those silent, padded sneakers on a basketball court. If you believe your abilities and intelligence are carved in stone, that's a fixed mindset playing tricks on you. It whispers that talent alone leads to success, and effort is for those who don't have enough of it. Sounds familiar? This mindset can be quite limiting in the world of sports — and life in general. It's like putting on a mental straitjacket that keeps you from moving freely towards improvement.

Imagine avoiding challenges because they threaten your self-image or giving up at the first sign of trouble because, deep down, you believe you don't have what it takes to improve. Or worse, feeling threatened by the success of others because it somehow makes you feel inferior. This mindset could turn the locker room into a theater of jealousy and insecurity, stifling not just your growth but also the team's dynamics.

Growth Mindset: Your Secret Weapon

Now, flip the script. Imagine embracing challenges like a surfer welcomes a giant wave — exciting opportunities to ride and master. A growth mindset thrives on effort, seeing it as the path to mastery. It understands that intelligence and talents are just the starting point and that these abilities can blossom through application and experience. This is the mindset that tells you, "Yes, you can learn it. Yes, you can improve."

This mindset fuels you to learn from criticism rather than avoiding it. Where a fixed mindset dodges feedback, a growth mindset invites it over for dinner and a chat. It's about stretching your personal boundaries, not proving you're shackled to them. And when you see others succeed, it's a chance to cheer them on and learn from their journeys, not a reason to harbor envy. In the sports arena, this means every practice, every game, and every interaction becomes a stepping stone to becoming a better version of yourself.

The Science Behind Mindset: Why It Matters

Let's get a bit scientific here. The concept of mindsets isn't just motivational poster material; it's backed by some serious psychology. Research by Dr. Carol Dweck, a pioneering psychologist in the field of motivation, demonstrates that the way we think about our abilities profoundly affects how we act and, thus, our overall performance. Her studies prove that people with a growth mindset are more likely to persevere when they fail because they don't believe failure is a permanent condition. They see it as a heart-pumping, thrilling part of the learning process.

Understanding this can fundamentally alter how you tackle your sports training. Instead of dreading challenges, you begin to seek them, knowing each hurdle jumped adds to your growth. Each failure turns from a stop sign to a detour sign on the road to success, guiding you to alternative paths and possibilities. This shift in perspective is like upgrading your mental software to a version that's wired to propel you forward, no matter the hurdles.

Exercise: Growth Mindset Journal

To put this into practice, start a Growth Mindset Journal. Each day, jot down moments when you felt stuck or challenged. Reflect on how you responded: Did you lean into the challenge, or did you back away? Write down three ways you could approach these situations differently next time, using a growth mindset. This exercise will not only help you recognize your own mindset patterns but also equip you with strategies to cultivate a stronger, more resilient approach to challenges.

1.2 Real-Life Examples: Athletes Who Transformed Their Game

Let's talk about Michael Jordan, a name synonymous not just with basketball greatness but with the epitome of a growth mindset in sports. Picture this: a young Jordan, teeming with passion but cut from his high school basketball team. Yes, you heard it right — cut. For many, this could have been the end of the road, a crushing blow to self-esteem and ambition. Instead, Jordan used this rejection as fuel for his fire. He didn't sulk or stew over the decision.

Instead, he hit the gym with a vengeance, practicing harder and pushing himself beyond the limits. His commitment to improvement was relentless, driven not by the desire to prove others wrong but to prove to himself that he could do it.

Through sheer perseverance, Jordan transformed his game, eventually making the team and soaring well beyond to become an NBA legend. It's not just his athletic prowess that made him a household name; it's his unyielding belief in the possibility of self-improvement. Each game, each season, was an opportunity to be better than the last. Even at the peak of his career, Jordan was known for his practice intensity and his dedication to refining every aspect of his game. This mindset, this unwavering commitment to growth, is what separates the good from the truly great.

Now, let's shift gears to Serena Williams, a titan in the world of tennis. Serena's journey is a powerful testament to resilience and continuous self-improvement. Over her illustrious career, she has faced numerous challenges, including serious injuries and personal setbacks that would have sidelined many athletes. However, Serena viewed each obstacle as a learning opportunity, a stepping stone to greater success. Her resilience is legendary. After a challenging loss or an injury, she returned to the court stronger and more determined, her gameplay honed from the lessons learned during recovery.

Her commitment to excellence is evident in her rigorous training regimen and her mental preparation. Serena has never been complacent; her career is a continuous quest for improvement, mastering the mental and physical aspects of tennis. This drive, rooted in a growth mindset, has kept her at the top of her game for years, making her one of the most formidable and respected athletes in sports history.

Lastly, consider Tom Brady, often referred to as the GOAT (Greatest of All Time) in NFL circles. Brady's professional start was far from glamorous. Selected as the 199th pick in the sixth round of the 2000 NFL draft, he began his career overlooked and underestimated. Yet, what he possessed was a profound work ethic and an unshakeable belief in his ability to improve. Brady spent countless hours studying game films, working on his technique, and understanding his opponents' strategies. His meticulous preparation and dedication to improvement are hallmarks of his career.

Brady's approach to football is cerebral; he analyzes every defeat and victory to fine-tune his strategies. Each game is a learning experience, a chance to refine his skills and adapt. This mindset has not only led to numerous Super Bowl victories but has also allowed him to play at an elite level well into his 40s, an age when most players have long retired. Brady's career is a clear illustration of how a growth mindset, combined with relentless dedication and strategic learning, can lead to extraordinary longevity and success in sports.

These athletes, each a legend in their own right, embody the principles of a growth mindset. They show us that setbacks can be springboards and that effort and dedication can transform potential into unmatched excellence. Their stories are not just about sports; they are about life. They teach us that no matter the field, the principles of perseverance, continuous learning, and resilience can guide us to our goals. Whether you're an aspiring athlete, a coach, a parent, or anyone striving to achieve a dream, remember: a growth or fixed mindset can quite literally make or break your success. Choose growth, choose resilience, choose relentless pursuit—and watch how far it takes you.

Chapter 2: The Confidence Code

Alright, let's talk about confidence. Not the "fake it 'til you make it" kind or the swagger that comes from wearing a new pair of sneakers, but the real, solid, unshakeable confidence that you can call upon whether you're at the free-throw line with one second on the clock or standing in front of your peers presenting a project. This kind of confidence isn't born overnight, nor does it come from other people's approval — it grows from within you, rooted in a deep understanding and acceptance of who you are, along with a clear recognition of your abilities.

2.1 Building Unshakeable Confidence

The Foundation of Confidence: It's an Inside Job

True confidence, the kind that sticks to your ribs like your grandmother's homemade lasagna, is all about self-belief. It's knowing in your bones that you're capable, competent, and worthy, regardless of the outcome. It's not about puffing your chest out and pretending to be something you're not. Not only that, it's deeper than that — it's about knowing yourself so well that external setbacks don't shake your core.

Think about the last time you tried something new. Maybe it was a new trick on the skateboard or a difficult problem in algebra. Initially, you might not have succeeded, but the confidence to try again didn't come from someone else patting you on the back (though that's always nice). It came from within, from a place that understands learning and growth are part of the game. This core self-assurance allows you to navigate both victories and losses without losing your sense of self.

Practices to Build Confidence: Small Steps Lead to Big Wins

Now, building this kind of confidence doesn't happen by just sitting around and wishing for it. It takes practice and a few strategic moves. Let's start with daily affirmations. These aren't just cheesy sayings your aunt posts on Facebook; they're powerful tools for mindset change. Each morning, try looking in the mirror and saying something positive about yourself, like "I am resilient" or "I handle challenges with grace." These affirmations reinforce your self-belief and gradually chip away at any self-doubt.

Next up, let's talk about setting and achieving small goals. Confidence builds when you see yourself progressing, so set small, achievable goals that lead you toward your bigger ambitions. Each small win is a building block for your confidence. Whether it's improving your time on the track or mastering a new study technique, celebrate these wins — no matter how small they may seem.

Visualization is another powerful tool. Spend a few minutes each day visualizing yourself succeeding in your activities. See yourself scoring the winning goal, acing the test, or nailing your dance routine. Feel the success, the applause, the high-fives. This mental rehearsal boosts your confidence by making your goals feel more attainable.

Role of Preparation: Confidence's Best Friend

One of the most effective ways to build confidence is through preparation. Think about it: the more you practice, the more familiar and skilled you become at an activity, and the more your confidence grows. It's like knowing the lyrics to your favorite song so well that you can sing it in your sleep. That level of familiarity and preparedness reduces anxiety and boosts self-assurance.

For athletes, this might mean extra hours spent in the gym or studying game films. For students, it involves reviewing notes and preparing for exams thoroughly. For anyone stepping into a new role or challenge, it means taking the time to learn about the expectations and required skills. Preparation doesn't just make you better at what you do; it makes you feel better about your ability to handle whatever comes your way.

Interactive Element: Confidence Building Exercise

To wrap up this section, let's put theory into action. I want you to try a simple exercise that combines these strategies. For the next week (yes - 7 days), start each day by writing down one small goal you aim to achieve by the end of the day. It could be anything from speaking up in class to trying a new workout. Then, spend a minute visualizing yourself achieving this goal. Finally, end your day by reflecting on your success and any lessons learned. This daily practice will boost your confidence and provide a clear track of your progress.

Building true confidence is about more than just feeling good at the moment. It's about establishing a lasting belief in yourself that persists through ups and downs. It's about knowing your worth, recognizing your abilities, and walking through life with a genuine sense of self-assurance that says, "I've got this." And trust me, you really do.

2.2 Overcoming Self-Doubt: Techniques and Strategies

Let's face it, self-doubt is like that uninvited guest at your party who just won't leave, no matter how many hints you drop. It sneaks up on you right when you're about to take a free throw or present your project in front of the class. But why does it show up, and more importantly, how can you show it the door? Understanding the roots of self-doubt and arming yourself with strategies to combat it can turn those uneasy feelings into powerful lessons in confidence.

Recognizing the Roots of Self-Doubt

Self-doubt often stems from a few usual suspects: fear of failure, the habit of comparing ourselves to others, and our experiences. Fear of failure can paralyze you, whispering in your ear that it's better not to try than to risk failing. Comparisons, on the other hand, can make you feel like you'll never stack up to your seemingly flawless peers or sports heroes. And let's not forget those past experiences — like that time you stumbled during a crucial play or flubbed a line in the school play—these memories can stick around, convincing you they'll repeat themselves.

To tackle self-doubt, start by recognizing these triggers. Keep a simple diary for a week and jot down moments when self-doubt creeps in. Note what's happening, how you feel, and what you're thinking. Spotting patterns helps you predict and prepare for these moments instead of being blindsided by them.

Flipping the Script on Negative Thoughts

Once you've got a handle on when and why self-doubt strikes, it's time to challenge it. This is where cognitive restructuring comes into play—a fancy term for changing your negative thoughts into positive ones. It starts with catching those pesky negative thoughts in the act. When you find yourself thinking, "I can't do this," pause. Reframe that thought to, "I'm nervous because I care, but I can handle this."

Here's a step-by-step exercise to sharpen this skill:

1. **Catch It**: Write down a negative thought when it appears.
2. **Check It**: Ask yourself, is this thought based on facts or feelings? Is there evidence that contradicts this thought?

3. **Change It**: Replace the negative thought with a more balanced or positive one.

Practice makes perfect. The more you practice cognitive restructuring, the more automatic it becomes. You'll start to notice that these negative thoughts lose their grip, and your mind becomes a much more positive space.

Cultivating a Garden of Positive Influences

Imagine trying to grow a plant in rocky soil. It's tough, right? The same goes for growing your confidence in rocky surroundings. Surrounding yourself with positive influences — people who support you, uplift you, and believe in you — can change the soil of your environment, making it rich and conducive to growth.

A positive support system includes coaches who encourage you, friends who cheer you on, and family members who believe in your abilities. These are the people who remind you of your strengths when self-doubt tries to make you forget them. They're also the ones who encourage you to keep going when things get tough. If your current circle isn't very supportive, it might be time to branch out. Join clubs, teams, or online communities where positivity and encouragement are the norms.

Building this network doesn't happen overnight, but each step you take towards surrounding yourself with positivity plants seeds of confidence that will grow over time. Remember, the right environment can turn a tiny seed of self-belief into a flourishing tree of confidence.

As we wrap up this exploration of overcoming self-doubt, remember that self-doubt is a common experience, but it doesn't have to be a permanent state. By understanding its triggers, challenging negative thoughts, and fostering a supportive environment, you're well on your way to turning doubt into a stepping stone rather than a stumbling block. These strategies aren't just about sports or school — they're about life. They equip you to handle whatever challenges come your way with a strong, confident mindset.

Moving forward, as you continue to apply these techniques, you'll find that self-doubt visits less frequently and stays for shorter periods. You'll be better prepared to face new challenges, embrace opportunities, and step into your greatness, no matter the arena. And that's something to look forward to as we continue to explore the building blocks of an unstoppable mindset in the chapters to come.

Chapter 3: Focus and Concentration

Welcome back! How did it go? Did you notice any progress? I am sure you did. Alright, let's zero in on something that might just be your secret weapon on the field, in the classroom, or frankly, any arena of life—focus. Imagine you're in the last crucial minutes of a game, the score is tied, and it's your move. The crowd is loud, the pressure's on, but there's a calmness inside you. Why? Because you've mastered the art of focus. You see, having laser-sharp focus is like having a superpower. It lets you block out the noise and, quite literally, focus on nailing that goal or acing that test. So, how do you develop this superpower? Let's dive into the nuts and bolts of building and maintaining razor-sharp focus.

3.1 Developing Laser-Sharp Focus

The Importance of Focus

Focus is the secret sauce to achieving peak performance. In the world of sports, it's what allows athletes to perform complex tasks with precision and react swiftly to changing situations on the field. Think of a quarterback scanning the field for an open receiver, or a tennis player anticipating their opponent's next move — what they have in common is incredible focus. This isn't just about narrowing your vision of the goal but also about maintaining a heightened state of awareness that allows you to absorb and process crucial information rapidly and accurately. When you're truly focused, your reactions aren't just quick — they're spot on.

CHAPTER 3: FOCUS AND CONCENTRATION

Training the Mind: Techniques to Sharpen Your Focus

Now, training your mind to focus might not sound as cool as lifting weights or sprinting, but believe me, it's equally, if not more, powerful. Let's start with mindfulness meditation. This is all about being present in the moment. By practicing mindfulness, you train your brain to concentrate on the here and now, keeping pesky distractions at bay. Here's a simple way to start:

- **Mindfulness Meditation**: Find a quiet spot and sit comfortably. Close your eyes and focus solely on your breathing. Inhale slowly, then exhale, paying attention to the rise and fall of your chest. When your mind starts to wander (and it will), gently guide your focus back to your breath. Start with just five minutes a day, and increase the time as you get more comfortable with the practice.

Next up, let's talk about concentration drills. These are exercises designed to enhance your ability to focus on a single task for extended periods. A fun and effective drill is the "ball toss."

- **Ball Toss Concentration Drill**: Grab a ball and a partner. Stand about five feet apart. Start tossing the ball to each other, slowly at first, then gradually increasing the speed. The goal is to maintain eye contact with the ball at all times, focusing intently on catching and throwing. It sounds simple, but it requires and builds great concentration.

Visualization is another powerful tool in your focus arsenal. It involves creating a mental image of yourself performing a task perfectly before you actually do it.

- **Visualization Practice**: Take a moment to close your eyes and imagine yourself in a game or during a performance. See yourself executing perfectly, each movement, each step. Feel the success and the positive emotions associated with it. This mental rehearsal primes your brain for actual performance, enhancing your focus when it counts.

Setting Clear Goals: The Focus Magnifier

Setting goals isn't just about defining what you want to achieve — it's about clarifying your focus. By setting specific, measurable, attainable, relevant, and time-bound (SMART) goals, you give your mind a clear target to focus on. This clarity reduces mental clutter and directs your cognitive resources toward achieving those goals. Think of your goals as a roadmap; without them, you're just wandering around hoping to stumble upon success.

- **Setting SMART Goals**: Start with something specific you want to achieve in your sport or studies. Let's say you aim to improve your free-throw accuracy in basketball. A SMART goal could be: "I want to increase my free-throw success rate from 70% to 80% by the end of this season by practicing free throws for 30 minutes each day." This goal is specific (increase free-throw accuracy), measurable (70% to 80%), attainable (a 10% increase is realistic), relevant (directly improves your game), and time-bound (by the end of the season).

Interactive Element: Goal-Setting Exercise

To put this into practice, try this simple exercise:

- **Goal-Setting Worksheet**: Create a chart of your long-term and short-term goals using the SMART framework. Divide them into categories like 'Sports', 'Academic', and 'Personal Development'. Under each, write down what you aim to achieve, how you'll measure your progress, the steps you'll take to get there, and the timeline you're giving yourself. Review and adjust these goals monthly.

By training your mind with mindfulness, engaging in concentration drills, visualizing success, and setting clear, structured goals, you're not just playing games — you're mastering them. With these tools, you'll find your focus sharpening, like turning the lens on a camera until the shot comes into clear view. And once you have that focus, there's very little you can't achieve.

3.2 Techniques to Eliminate Distractions

Let's face it, distractions are like those annoying gnats that just won't leave you alone during a summer barbecue. They buzz around, relentlessly trying to divert your attention from the task at hand. In the realm of sports and life, distractions can take many forms, from the internal chatter in your mind to the buzz of a smartphone. Mastering the art of cutting through these distractions is crucial, not just for athletes, but for anyone aiming to stay on top of their game. So, how do you swat those pesky distractions away? Let's break it down.

Identifying Distractions: Your Personal Bug Spray

Before you can tackle distractions, you need to know what they are. Sounds straightforward, right? But often, we're not even aware of what's pulling our focus away. Distractions generally fall into two categories: internal and external. Internal distractions include those nagging thoughts about upcoming exams, replaying that awkward thing you said at lunch, or worrying about the results of a game. External distractions? They're all around — from the ping of a text message to side conversations happening near you while you're trying to focus.

The first step to managing these is simple: recognition. **Keep a distraction journal for a few days.** Every time you find yourself losing focus, jot down what snagged your attention. Was it a thought, a noise, or maybe something visual? You might start to notice patterns like perhaps you get distracted by social media notifications or start daydreaming about weekend plans during practice. Knowing your main distractors is like knowing what kind of bait the gnats like; once you know, you can start avoiding it.

Creating a Focus-Friendly Environment: Build Your Fortress

Think of your focus as a fortress—you want to fortify it against invaders (a.k.a. distractions). Start with your physical environment. Is your study or practice area cluttered? A messy space can lead to a messy mind. Take some time to declutter. Organize your gear, tidy up your workspace, and create a setup that's conducive to concentration. This doesn't mean your space has to be stark and boring — just organized in a way that minimizes distractions.

Next, think about establishing routines. Routine is like armor for your focus fortress. It helps your brain know when it's time to concentrate. This could be a pre-practice ritual that includes stretching, listening to a particular playlist, or reviewing your goals for the session. Routines signal to your brain, "Hey, it's time to dial in."

Don't forget about using tools and tech to your advantage. Apps that block social media during set hours can help you avoid digital distractions. Noise-canceling headphones are great for drowning out background noise. Use technology as a gatekeeper, not as a distraction.

Staying Present: The Art of Focus

Now, let's talk about staying in the moment. This is crucial during both practice and competition. Techniques like deep breathing exercises help anchor you in the now. Try this: breath in for four counts, hold for four, exhort for four, and wait for four before taking another breath. This is called breathing in a "square". This technique can center your mind and body, pushing distractions to the periphery.

Mental cues are also powerful tools. These are short, easy-to-remember phrases that bring your focus back to the task. Phrases like "eyes on the ball" or "smooth and steady" can work wonders. Find a cue that resonates with you and use it whenever you feel your attention waning.

Lastly, let's talk about achieving a state of flow, the ultimate level of focus where the world falls away, and it's just you and the game. Flow happens when you're fully engaged in what you're doing, when the challenge of the task matches your skill level perfectly. While you can't force flow, you can cultivate the conditions that make it more likely. This means setting clear goals, seeking immediate feedback on your performance, and choosing tasks that challenge you without overwhelming you.

By identifying your distractions, creating a focus-friendly environment, and practicing techniques to stay present, you're well on your way to maintaining sharp focus, no matter the pressures around you. These strategies are tools in your toolkit, ready to help you cut through the noise and stay dialed in.

As we wrap up this chapter on focus and concentration, remember that the battle against distractions is ongoing. It's about recognizing what interrupts your focus, creating an environment that helps sustain it, and mastering the mental techniques that allow you to stay present in any situation. These skills are not only vital in sports but are transferable to every aspect of life, helping you to maintain clarity and purpose in the face of any challenge. Ready to move on? In the next chapter, we'll explore resilience, the backbone of mental toughness, and how you can build it to withstand any setbacks you might face. Keep your eyes on the prize, and let's keep pushing forward.

Now, before you continue with this book - put this book down for a week (yes - it is still 7 days) and concentrate on the following daily routine instead:

1) Stick a note on your bathroom mirror that says, "Say something positive about yourself to yourself!" and do just that for 7 days straight.

2) Put a small notebook that you have written the title "Growth Mindset Journal" on and a pen on your bedside table. Start each day by writing down one small goal you aim to achieve by the end of the day in the journal.

3) Then, spend a minute (get an egg clock to put beside your notebook and pen) visualizing yourself achieving this goal. Come on - it is only 60 seconds we are talking about.

4) Bring your journal with you as a reminder and:

a) **Catch It**: Write down a negative thought when it appears.

b) **Check It**: Ask yourself if this thought is based on facts or feelings. Is there evidence that contradicts this thought?

c) **Change It**: Replace the negative thought with a more balanced or positive one.

5) Finally, end your day before going to sleep by reflecting on your success and any lessons learned. Be sure to note them down in your journal.

a) Did you have any moments that day when you felt stuck or challenged?

b) How did you respond? Did you lean into the challenge, or did you back away?

c) Then, write down three ways you can approach these situations differently next time, using a growth mindset.

6) Also, don't forget to celebrate your wins — no matter how small they may seem. Pat yourself on the back. Praise yourself when you succeed, or why not buy yourself a bar of chocolate to reward yourself?

7) Now, 3 days into this daily routine - add the Distraction journaling during the remaining 4 days. Every time you find yourself losing focus, put down what snagged your attention. Was it a thought, a noise, or maybe something visual?

CHAPTER 3: FOCUS AND CONCENTRATION

When you have done this for 7 days, you are welcome back to pick this book up again. Consider this as a "warm-up" period before what's to come...

I should also mention here before you dive headfirst into your 30-Day Challenge that you can also use the "Mindset Companion for Teen Athletes: Growth Mindset Journal – Will you Face Your 30-Day Challenge" instead of a notebook. You will find it on Amazon.

MENTAL TOUGHNESS FOR TEEN ATHLETES

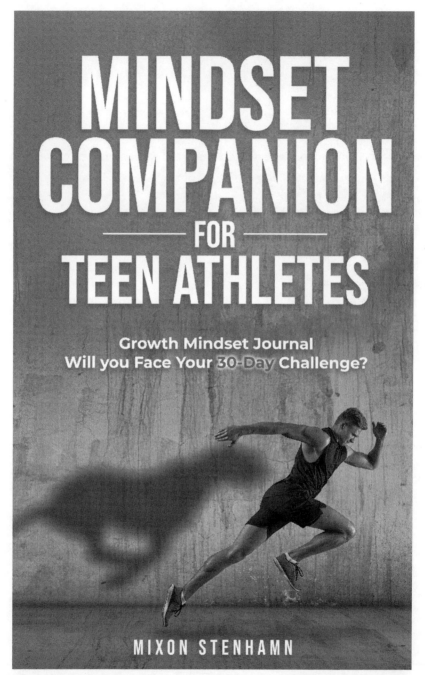

This is the Companion Journal to this Book you can find on Amazon to facilitate your journaling through your 30-Day Challenge.

II

Part 2: Daily Drills – Your 30-Day Action Plan

Week 1: Setting the Foundation

Alright, strap in, and let's get the ball rolling—or should I say, let's get the goals rolling? Because that's what Week 1 is all about laying down the foundational stones for a fortress of success. And no, we're not talking about medieval castles here, though that would be cool. We're talking about building a mental framework that supports and guides you toward your ultimate victories, be they on the field, in the classroom, or even in your personal life. So, grab your mental bricks and mortar, and let's start constructing!

Day 1: Goal Setting and Visualization

Goal Setting: Your Blueprint for Success

Imagine you're setting out on a road trip. You wouldn't just fill up the gas tank, pack a bag of snacks, and then just drive off into the sunset without a destination, right? Well, setting goals is like inputting your desired destination into your GPS. It gives you a clear direction and endpoint. But not just any goals—SMART goals. Yes, they're actually smart, and here's how:

- **Specific**: Clear and concise. Like deciding whether you're shooting hoops or scoring goals.
- **Measurable**: You need to know when you've arrived, right? Like knowing you need to score 30 points in a game.
- **Achievable**: Be real—aiming to fly by flapping your arms might not work

out.
- **Relevant**: Your goals should align with your bigger game plan. Think about what's really important to your success.
- **Time-bound**: Set a deadline. Without one, it's like setting off on that road trip thinking you'll get there eventually, but when?

Now, why write these goals down? There's magic in the act of writing. It's like signing a contract with yourself. It makes the goals stick, both in your mind and in reality. Make it a daily ritual—scribble down your goals every night before you sleep and every morning when you wake up. It keeps your objectives clear and your motivation fresh.

Visualization: See It, Then Be It

Now, onto visualization. This isn't about daydreaming you're a superhero (though feel free to do that in your spare time). It's about mentally rehearsing your success. Athletes like LeBron James and Serena Williams swear by this technique. They see themselves winning before they even step onto the court. Here's how you can do it too:

1. **Find a Quiet Spot**: Eliminate distractions. This is your mental gym.
2. **Breathe and Relax**: Take deep breaths. Calm your mind because a relaxed mind is a receptive mind.
3. **Picture Your Goal**: Start with the end in mind. See yourself achieving your goal. Make it as detailed as possible. Where are you, who's there, and what does it feel like?
4. **Walk Through the Steps**: Now, mentally, walk through the critical steps leading to that goal. If it's a basketball game, see yourself making those shots. If it's a test, see yourself recalling the information flawlessly.
5. **Feel the Success**: Don't just see it; feel it. The excitement, the pride, the joy—let those emotions flood through you.

Practice this regularly. Over time, these mental rehearsals will build your confidence and transform your inner vision into outer reality. Remember, the mind can't distinguish well between what's vividly imagined and what's real, so make those mental images vivid!

Visual Aid: Guided Visualization Track

Consider using a guided visualization audio track. These are designed to lead you through the process, often enhancing the experience and making it easier to envision your success. They act like a GPS for your goals—guiding you through the mental landscapes of your achievements.

As you wrap up Day 1 of this foundational week, remember that setting SMART goals and practicing visualization aren't just exercises—they're critical tools that equip you for the journey ahead. They are your map and compass in the wilderness of competition and challenge. As you continue with the rest of the week's activities, keep referring back to your goals and the vivid images of your success—they are the anchors that will keep you focused and driven, no matter how rough the seas get.

This day's Goal: Your SMART Goals are written down in your Journal, and Corresponding Visualizations are pictured at least once.

Day 2: Positive Affirmations

The Power of Words: Rewiring Your Brain for Success

Let's chat about the magic of positive affirmations and how they can literally change the game for you. Picture this: every thought you have is a little nudge in your brain's wiring, pushing you toward a specific behavior and outcome. Now, what if you could control those nudges? That's where positive affirmations come into play. They're not just feel-good quotes or motivational posters; they're powerful statements that can reinforce your self-worth and objectives, effectively reprogramming your mind toward success.

Here's the science bit: your brain loves patterns and often follows the path of least resistance, which means it will continue to think in a way that it's been conditioned to think. If that path is riddled with self-doubt and negativity, guess where you're heading? Yep, not towards the winner's podium. However, when you consistently feed it positive, affirming thoughts, you start creating new neural pathways. This process, known as neuroplasticity, is your brain's ability to reorganize itself by forming new neural connections throughout life. So, by practicing positive affirmations, you're basically sculpting your brain's structure towards a more positive mindset.

Think of affirmations as mental exercise. Just as you train your body to run faster or jump higher, you train your mind to think in a way that supports your ambitions and values. This mental conditioning can boost your confidence, reduce feelings of anxiety before a big game or test, and even increase your resilience to stress. It's like building a mental muscle that helps you lift the weights of daily challenges with ease.

Creating Personal Affirmations: Tailor-Made for Your Success

Crafting your own personal affirmations is like creating a custom playlist that gets you pumped up or winds you down — each statement should resonate with you personally and relate to your specific goals and challenges. Here's how you can create affirmations that aren't just words, but catalysts for change:

1. **Identify Your Goals and Challenges**: What are you working towards? What obstacles are in your way? Your affirmations should address these directly. If confidence in your athletic performance is your goal, an affirmation could be, "I am strong, skilled, and confident."
2. **Keep It Positive and Present Tense**: Always phrase your affirmations in the present tense and ensure they're positive. Instead of saying, "I will not be anxious," say, "I am calm and focused." This tricks your brain into believing that the desired state is currently true.

3. **Make It Believable**: If your affirmation feels too far-fetched, it's going to be hard to really embrace it. Start with something you can genuinely believe. For instance, if you're new to a sport, instead of saying, "I am the best player," try, "I am improving with every practice."
4. **Add an Emotional Charge**: Emotions amplify the impact of your affirmations. Include how achieving this goal will make you feel. For example, "I feel proud and energized when I improve my personal best."

Daily Practice: Incorporating Affirmations into Your Routine

Consistency is key when it comes to affirmations. They work best when integrated into your daily routine, turning positive thinking into a habit. Here are some practical ways to make affirmations a part of your everyday life:

- **Morning Pep-Talk**: Start your day by repeating your affirmations out loud. Stand in front of the mirror, look yourself in the eyes, and say them with conviction. This boosts your confidence and sets a positive tone for the day. It is hard to remember to do? Just add a post-it on the bathroom mirror.
- **Write Them Down**: Keep a journal of affirmations. Write them down every morning or night. This not only reinforces the affirmations but also makes them more tangible. Seeing them in your own handwriting makes them more personal and real.
- **Warm-Up Wisely**: Before practice or games, use affirmations to get in the right mental space. Repeat them during stretches or warm-ups. This can help reduce performance anxiety and increase focus.
- **Reminders and Alerts**: Set reminders on your phone to pop up throughout the day with your affirmations. Each reminder is a mini mental reset, steering you back to a positive and empowered mindset.

By making affirmations a regular part of your life, you're not just hoping for change; you're actively wiring your brain for success. Whether it's before a big game, during a tough workout, or while studying for an exam, these powerful statements serve as reminders of your strengths, goals, and the fact that you have the power to shape your own outcomes. So, let's keep moving forward and turn those positive words into positive actions.

This Daily Goal: Your Personal Affirmations are written down in your Journal and performed at least once.

Day 3: Understand Your Strengths and Weaknesses

When you're aiming to play your best game, whether on the court, in the field, or at your desk, knowing your toolkit is crucial. Think of yourself as a Swiss Army knife. Sure, that corkscrew might not be handy during a basketball game, but the screwdriver could be just what you need to tighten a loose hoop before a game-winning shot. Today's focus? Digging deep into that toolkit to identify which tools — your strengths — are already sharp and shiny, and which ones — your weaknesses — could use a bit of oiling or a complete overhaul.

Self-Assessment: Your Personal Inventory

Let's kick off with a bit of self-assessment. This isn't about patting yourself on the back for what you're good at and beating yourself up for where you fall short. It's about honest evaluation and strategic development. Here's a simple way to start: Grab a notebook (we will use up plenty of notebooks...), find a quiet spot, and ask yourself some pointed questions like, "What parts of my game (or skill set) feel almost effortless?" and "When do I feel most challenged or out of my depth?" Write down your thoughts. It's important to do this in a space where you feel relaxed and unhurried because the best insights come when you're not under pressure.

Next, let's formalize this a bit. You can create a two-column chart. Label one column "Strengths" and the other "Areas for Improvement." Under strengths, jot down all the skills or qualities you feel confident about. These could range from physical abilities like speed or endurance to mental skills like staying calm under pressure or being a good team player. In the areas for improvement column, be honest about where you feel less confident. Maybe it's your three-point shot, your ability to stay focused under stress, or even managing time effectively.

To deepen this self-assessment, consider asking for feedback from coaches, teammates, or anyone who regularly observes your performance. Sometimes, others see things in us that we might overlook. Incorporate their insights into your chart. This exercise isn't just a one-off; revisit and update it regularly. As you evolve, so will your strengths and areas for improvement.

Building on Strengths: Play to Your Advantages

Now, focusing on your strengths doesn't mean just basking in them — it means leveraging them to maximize your performance. For instance, if one of your strengths is your explosive speed, how can you use that more effectively during a game? Could you refine your start to make those first few steps even quicker? Or if you're praised for your strategic thinking in business, how can you use that to foresee and mitigate risks in projects you manage?

Look at elite athletes like basketball player Stephen Curry. Known for his incredible shooting skills, Curry doesn't rest on his laurels. He continually works on perfecting his shot from different angles and under various game conditions. What's your "shot"? How can you make it even better? Sometimes, it's about finding new ways to apply an existing strength. If you're a great communicator, for instance, perhaps you can take on a leadership role in team discussions or help mediate conflicts.

Addressing Weaknesses: Turning Liabilities into Assets

Confronting your weaknesses can be daunting, but remember, every weakness is an opportunity for growth. The first step is to pick one area to focus on at a time. Trying to fix everything at once is like trying to juggle six balls when you've only just mastered three — you're setting yourself up to drop them all.

Once you've chosen one area to improve, set specific, achievable goals for development. If improving your endurance is the goal, you might start by adding an extra day of cardio to your training schedule each week. Break it down into manageable steps. Then, seek feedback on your progress. This could be through a coach monitoring your training or even using tech tools like apps that track athletic performance or productivity tools for workplace tasks.

Practice drills are your best friend here. For athletic weaknesses, drills that target specific skills can be incredibly effective. An example, if dribbling is a weak spot, daily dribbling exercises can help. Regarding mental or strategic weaknesses, simulation exercises or role-play scenarios can be beneficial. The key is consistent practice and regular review of your progress.

Today's efforts in understanding your strengths and weaknesses are about building a more complete, more competent you. Whether it's leveraging your quick decision-making skills to take advantage of fast-breaking opportunities in a game or honing your project management skills to ensure your team meets its deadlines, every step you take in self-assessment, building on strengths, and addressing weaknesses is a step toward becoming a more rounded and skilled individual. Keep pushing, keep assessing, and keep optimizing. The best version of yourself awaits just around the corner.

The goal of this day: Your Strengths & Weaknesses written down in your Journal together with Improvement Goals and how to achieve them.

Day 4: Develop a Routine

Imagine your favorite athlete. Now picture them on a day of a big game. What do you think their morning looks like? Are they scrambling around, searching for their gear, skipping breakfast, and just winging it? Or do you see them following a set pattern, a routine that's been tweaked to perfection, ensuring they're as ready as they can be, both mentally and physically? I'd bet on the latter. That's because routines are powerful. Like a well-oiled machine, a good routine ensures everything runs smoothly, reducing stress and sharpening focus. Here's why sticking to a routine can be a game-changer for your performance.

The Role of Routine: Your Performance Enhancer

Routines are like psychological signals. They tell your brain, "Hey, it's time to switch gears." This is crucial, especially when you want to transition from 'relax mode' to 'high-performance mode'. For athletes, this could mean rituals before a game, like wearing a particular pair of socks, listening to a specific pump-up song, or even a special handshake with a teammate. These rituals, part of a broader routine, help in reducing performance anxiety. They create a familiar pattern in your day, which can be incredibly comforting when nerves start to kick in. Moreover, a solid routine enhances focus by minimizing the mental clutter caused by last-minute decisions or distractions. When your day is structured, your mind isn't bogged down by chaos; instead, it's laser-focused on the tasks at hand.

Creating Your Routine: Tailoring Your Daily Blueprint

Crafting a routine that suits your needs can feel a bit like being a DJ—mixing and matching elements until you find that perfect beat. Here's how you can create a routine that hits all the right notes for you:

1. **Start with the essentials**: What are the non-negotiables in your day?

These could include school or work hours, training sessions, meals, and sleep. Plot these out on a timeline.
2. **Incorporate mental exercises**: Just like you train your body, your mind needs its workout too. Dedicate time for mental training practices like visualization or meditation. Even 10 minutes can make a big difference.
3. **Fuel right**: Include meal times that sync with your energy needs. This means not just eating at the right times but eating the right foods that will sustain you through your activities.
4. **Rest**: Yes, rest is a part of your routine. Ensure you have short breaks throughout the day and a proper wind-down ritual at night to get enough sleep.
5. **Flexibility**: Life isn't predictable. A good routine has built-in flexibility. Maybe it's a longer lunch on days when your mornings are intense, or a lighter training day if you're feeling under the weather.

For inspiration, look at successful athletes. Michael Phelps, for instance, famously visualizes his races every morning. This mental rehearsal is as much a part of his routine as his physical training. Similarly, Serena Williams starts her day with meditation, aligning her mind for the challenges ahead. These routines aren't just about physical preparation; they encompass mental and emotional readiness as well.

Sticking to Your Routine: Keeping the Rhythm Going

Now, maintaining a routine, especially a new one, can be as challenging as starting it. Here are some tips to keep you on track:

- **Consistency is key**: The more you stick to your routine, the more it becomes a habit. Over time, it will feel less like a chore and more like a regular part of your day.
- **Track your progress**: Keep a journal or use an app to track how well you're sticking to your routine. Seeing your success in writing can be a huge motivator.

- **Adjust as needed**: Be honest about what's working and what isn't. If you find you're consistently skipping a part of your routine, ask yourself why. Maybe it needs to be tweaked or timed differently.
- **Plan for disruptions**: Life happens—sick days, unexpected assignments, family events. Have a backup plan for when your routine is disrupted. Maybe swap your morning workout for an evening one, or do a shorter home-based exercise if you can't make it to the gym.
- **Reward yourself**: Small rewards can make sticking to your routine more appealing. Treat yourself to a movie night after a week of diligently following your routine, or indulge in your favorite snack after a particularly challenging day.

As you continue to develop and refine your routine, remember that it's a tool to help you perform your best. It's not meant to be a rigid set of rules that adds stress to your life. The right routine feels like a supportive friend, one that knows exactly what you need and when you need it, ensuring you're always game-ready, focused, and less anxious. Whether you're preparing for a championship game or a crucial exam, your routine is your secret weapon. So, tune it to fit your life's unique rhythm and watch how it transforms your performance, one day at a time.

Today's Goal: Your Daily Routine written down in your Journal to be refined continuously in eternity...

Day 5: The Importance of Sleep and Recovery

Sleep and Performance: Why Zzz's Are Your New Best Friend

Picture this: you're training hard, eating right, and you've got your eyes set on smashing personal records. But there's one crucial piece of the puzzle that might be slipping through the cracks — your sleep. Yes, those precious hours of shut-eye are more than just a chance to dream about winning championships; they're a cornerstone of athletic performance and recovery.

Let's dive into the science of sleep. When you sleep, your body goes into maintenance mode. This is the time when the magic of recovery happens. Human Growth Hormone (HGH), which is vital for tissue growth and repair, is released during deep sleep. This means the muscle tears from today's grueling training session are repaired while you're snoozing, making you stronger and ready for tomorrow's challenges.

But it's not just about muscles. Sleep is like a spa treatment for your brain. It helps consolidate memories, including those related to motor skills. So, that new dribbling technique or volleyball serve you're trying to master? Sleep helps cement those skills into your brain's "muscle memory." Additionally, adequate sleep regulates mood and cognitive functions, helping you stay sharp, make quick decisions on the field, and maintain a positive mindset.

Now, have you ever noticed how everything feels more challenging when you're tired? That's because sleep deprivation can significantly impair your physical performance. Studies have shown that lack of sleep can lead to decreased reaction times, reduced endurance, and a general feeling of lethargy. Plus, it can increase your susceptibility to injuries. So, if you're skimping on sleep, you're not just facing a groggy morning; you're potentially sidelining your athletic career.

Optimizing Sleep: Creating a Dream-Worthy Environment

Getting quality sleep is an art, and like any art, it requires a bit of technique and practice. Here are some tips to help you master it:

- **Establish a Bedtime Routine**: Just as you have a warm-up routine before games, create a wind-down routine before bed. This could involve reading a book, doing some gentle stretching, or listening to calming music. The key is consistency. Over time, this routine will signal to your body that it's time to power down, making it easier to fall asleep.
- **Craft a Sleep-Friendly Environment**: Evaluate your sleep environment.

Is it conducive to rest? Make sure your bedroom is cool, quiet, and dark. Invest in a good quality mattress and pillows—they're the unsung heroes in the quest for better sleep. Consider blackout curtains to block out light, and if noise is an issue, a white noise machine can be a game-changer.
- **Manage Stress**: Stress and sleep are like oil and water — they don't mix well. If you find your mind racing with tomorrow's to-do list, try some relaxation techniques like deep breathing or meditation before bed. Keeping a 'worry journal' where you jot down your thoughts can also help clear your mind and improve your sleep quality.

Active Recovery: Not Just Sitting on the Sidelines

Rest days are often misunderstood. Many athletes fear that taking a day off might set them back. However, active recovery is a critical component of any training regimen. It allows your body to recuperate without being completely idle, which can actually speed up the recovery process.

- **Stretching**: Incorporate light stretching into your recovery days to keep the blood flowing and help alleviate muscle tightness. Focus on dynamic stretches that mimic the movement patterns of your sport.
- **Foam Rolling**: This can be a godsend for sore muscles. Foam rolling helps break up scar tissue and improve blood flow to specific areas, aiding in the recovery and improving range of motion.
- **Light Activity**: Consider activities that are low impact and different from your regular training. If you're a runner, maybe a gentle swim or a leisurely bike ride. This keeps your body moving, and your mind engaged without the intensity of regular training sessions.

A Recovery Plan to Swear By

Creating a structured recovery plan is just as important as planning your workouts. Designate at least one day a week to focus solely on recovery techniques. Combine stretching, foam rolling, and light activities to keep the recovery process active. Also, ensure you're getting at least 7–9 hours of sleep per night — it's non-negotiable if you want to perform at your best.

Embracing recovery and sleep as integral parts of your training will not only enhance your physical capabilities but also protect you from burnout and injuries. Think of sleep and recovery as your secret weapons in achieving peak performance. By giving them the attention they deserve, you're setting the stage for a healthier, stronger, and more resilient athlete. So tonight, when you tuck yourself in, remember that each hour of sleep is a step towards your goals, a badge of honor in your quest for excellence.

Goal today: A Bedtime Routine & a Recovery Plan noted down in you Journal and the Bedtime Routine performed for the first time.

Day 6: Nutrition and Hydration for Optimal Performance

When you're gearing up for a big game or just pushing through a grueling training session, what you fuel your body with can be as crucial as the training itself. Think of your body as a high-performance vehicle. You wouldn't dream of throwing in low-grade fuel and expecting top-notch performance, right? That's where understanding the basics of nutrition and hydration comes into play, turning good athletes into great ones with stamina and power that lasts.

Fueling the Body: The Basics of Nutrition

Let's break it down simply: your body needs a mix of macronutrients and micronutrients to perform at its best. Macronutrients are the big three: carbohydrates, proteins, and fats. Each plays a unique role in your body. Carbohydrates are your body's main energy source. When you consume carbs, your body breaks them down into glucose, fueling everything you do, from sprinting to thinking. Good sources? Think whole grains, fruits, and veggies, not just bread and pasta. Next up, proteins, which are crucial for muscle repair and growth. After a heavy workout, your muscles are like a city after Godzilla's visit—protein is the construction crew that helps rebuild. Lean meats, fish, beans, and legumes are your go-to here. And let's not forget fats. They often get a bad rap, but healthy fats, like those found in avocados, nuts, and certain oils, are key for long-term energy, helping absorb vitamins and protect your vital organs.

Now, micronutrients—vitamins and minerals—might seem less significant because you need them in smaller amounts, but they're like the hidden bolts in a machine. Tiny but mighty, they keep the body functioning smoothly. Iron, for example, helps transport oxygen to your muscles, crucial during a high-octane match or a long run, while calcium builds strong bones to withstand the physical demands of sports.

Creating a Nutrition Plan: Your Personal Eating Playbook

Crafting a nutrition plan isn't about strict eating regimes or depriving yourself. It's about balance and making sure your body gets what it needs when it needs it. Start with timing your meals to support your training schedule. A hearty breakfast can kickstart your metabolism and fuel your morning activities. Include carbohydrates for energy and protein for muscle repair. Pre-workout meals should be lighter but still packed with carbs and some protein. Think a banana with a spoonful of peanut butter or a small yogurt parfait.

Post-workout is when your body is desperate for nutrients to start the repair process. Here, a mix of carbs and protein is vital. A smoothie with fruits, protein powder, and a dash of healthy fats from seeds or nuts can be a perfect recovery meal. And hydration? Water is your best friend. Staying hydrated helps maintain your performance, keeps joints lubricated, and helps transport nutrients to give you energy. During workouts, sip water regularly, and after, make sure you rehydrate adequately, especially if you sweat a lot.

Meal planning can be a game-changer here. Spend some time each week planning your meals. This helps you stay on track and reduces the temptation to grab something less optimal just because it's convenient. Think about preparing batches of meals that balance macros and micros effectively, so you always have a performance-enhancing meal ready when you need it.

Avoiding Pitfalls: Navigating Common Nutritional Mistakes

Even with the best intentions, there are common traps many athletes fall into. Skipping meals is a big one. It might seem like a time-saver, but missing meals can lead to reduced energy levels, slower reaction times, and even overeating later. Then there's not drinking enough fluids. Dehydration can sneak up on you, leading to decreased performance, fatigue, and muscle cramps. Keep a water bottle handy and sip throughout the day, not just when you're thirsty. Another misstep is relying on sports drinks excessively. While they can help replenish electrolytes during extended activities, they're often high in sugars and calories, which might not be necessary for your specific activity level.

Understanding and navigating these nutritional nuances can significantly impact your performance and overall health. By fueling your body correctly, you ensure that each training session, each game, and each day is powered by the best possible energy source. So, take control of your diet like you take control of the ball or your performance on the field, and watch as your game, and your health, reach new heights.

Today's Goal: Your Eating Playbook is documented in your Journal and a Shopping List based on the Playbook provided to your peers.

Day 7: Rest and Reflection

The Importance of Rest: Recharging for Resilience

Let's discuss a superpower that you might be underestimating: rest. Yes, in a world that glorifies the 'go-getter', dialing back and doing 'nothing' can sometimes feel like you're slacking off. But here's the kicker - rest isn't about doing nothing. It's about doing what's necessary for your body and mind to recover, regenerate, and come back stronger. Think of it this way: if you were driving a car non-stop, eventually it would overheat or run out of gas. Your body is no different. Continuous training without proper rest can lead to burnout, decreased performance, and even injuries.

Incorporating rest days into your training regimen isn't a sign of weakness; it's a strategy for sustainable strength. These are the days when the magic of muscle repair happens when your energy stores are replenished, and, importantly, when your mental stamina gets a reboot. This doesn't mean you flop onto the couch and binge-watch your favorite series—although occasionally, that's perfectly fine, too. Active rest can include lighter, non-competitive activities that keep the blood flowing but don't strain your body. Think leisurely walks, a gentle yoga session, or even some meditative breathing exercises. These activities help maintain your mobility and keep your mind engaged without the high stakes of intense training sessions.

Reflection Practices: Mirrors to Your Progress

Now, while your body is taking a well-deserved breather, what about your mind? This is where reflection swoops in. Reflection is about looking back with a purpose—analyzing what you've done, understanding why you did it, and thinking about how it can be done better. It's a powerful tool for personal growth that can transform good athletes into great ones, and it starts with a simple habit: can you guess? Yes, journaling.

Here's how you can integrate this into your routine. Keep a weekly reflection journal. At the end of each week, take some time to jot down what went well and what didn't. Ask yourself some probing questions: What were my biggest challenges this week? Did I meet the goals I set on Day 1? What lessons did I learn that I can apply moving forward? Writing these down isn't just about record-keeping; it's about self-dialogue and discovery. It helps you see patterns in your behavior, recognize your triggers, and pinpoint areas of improvement.

Planning Ahead: Charting the Course

Reflection gives you insights, but what should you do with them? That's where planning steps in. Using the insights from your reflection, start setting your intentions for the upcoming week. This is more than just goal-setting; this is strategic planning, taking into account not only what you hope to achieve but also what potential obstacles might arise and how you might overcome them.

Begin with reviewing the goals you set at the start of the week. Which ones did you hit? Which ones did you miss? Understanding why something wasn't achieved is as crucial as setting the goal in the first place. Maybe you aimed too high and needed to adjust the steps, or perhaps unexpected challenges threw you off course. Adjust your goals for the next week accordingly.

Then, prep mentally for the upcoming challenges. Visualize the week ahead. Imagine tackling your tasks with success. See yourself navigating potential setbacks with ease. This mental preparation sets a positive tone and arms you with confidence.

Finally, remember that flexibility is key. Life is unpredictable, and being too rigid in your plans can lead to frustration. Allow room for adjustments. Maybe set a couple of 'flex goals' that can be tackled if time and energy allow, but aren't critical if left for another time.

As you wrap up today's chapter on rest and reflection, carry with you the understanding that these elements are not just add-ons to your training; they are integral parts of it. They ensure that as you build your physical strength and skill, your mental resilience and strategic thinking are being nurtured too. This holistic approach not only prepares you for the sports arena but equips you with life skills that transcend the playing field.

Next week, we dive deeper into specific techniques and strategies that will help further develop and fine-tune your mental toughness. Each day will bring new tools and insights, each designed to build on the foundation we've laid this week. So, take today to rest and reflect, then come back ready to tackle the next set of challenges head-on.

Goal of the day: A weekly reflection page in your Journal together with your intentions for the upcoming week.

Week 2: Building Momentum

Hey there, superstar! So, you've made it through the first week, and I bet you're feeling a bit more like the captain of your ship — steady and ready. Now, let's add some wind to those sails and really get moving. This week, we're ratcheting things up a notch. We're going to tackle some of the trickier elements that can throw you off your game and learn how to dance in the rain, metaphorically speaking. Let's kick off with something that every athlete needs to master, regardless of their sport or level: managing fear and anxiety. Yes, those pesky feelings that can either fuel you or freeze you. Ready to turn them into your allies? Let's dive deep!

Day 8: Overcoming Fear and Anxiety

Understanding Fear and Anxiety

First off, let's get one thing straight—feeling fear and anxiety is as normal as sweating in a game. It's your body's natural response to perceived threats, and it can actually be quite helpful. Think of it as your internal alarm system, a kind of early warning radar that signals when you need to be on your toes. But here's the kicker: it's all about perception. Your brain might sometimes see a big game or a public performance as a saber-toothed tiger, which, let's be honest, it isn't.

Athletes often face fears like the fear of failure, the dread of injury, or just plain old performance anxiety. Physiologically, these fears can trigger your fight-or-flight response, releasing stress hormones like cortisol and adrenaline that can jack up your heart rate, make your palms sweaty, and sometimes blank out your mind. Psychologically, they can mess with your confidence and throw a wrench in your focus.

Techniques to Overcome Fear

Now, for the cool part — turning the tables on these fears. Let's start with some handy techniques:

- **Deep Breathing Exercises**: This is like hitting the reset button on your body's stress response. Try the 4-4-8 technique. Breathe in deeply through your nose for 4 seconds, hold that breath for 4 seconds, then exhale slowly through your mouth for 8 seconds. This helps reduce the panic mode and tells your brain, "Hey, relax, we got this."
- **Progressive Muscle Relaxation (PMR)**: This technique reduces the physical tension that fear can bring. Start by tensing a group of muscles as you breathe in, hold them tight for a few seconds, and then release them as you breathe out. Work your way through your body from your toes to your head. It's like giving your body a mini massage.
- **Cognitive Reframing**: Here's where you challenge those doom-and-gloom thoughts. Replace thoughts like "I'm going to mess up" with "I'm prepared and ready to do my best". It's about seeing the glass as half full, not just of water, but of opportunity.

Building Confidence

All these techniques are great, but they're even more powerful when combined with solid preparation and practice. The more prepared you are, the less room there is for fear to take root. Keep honing your skills, understanding your playbooks, and visualizing your success. This not only builds muscle memory but also fortifies your mental game.

Speaking of mental game, keep those positive affirmations in your toolkit.

Remind yourself of your strengths, your past successes, and your goals. Reinforce your self-belief every day because at the end of the day, confidence is your shield against the arrows of fear and anxiety.

So, as you step into the rest of the week, carry these strategies with you. Practice them, refine them, and make them a part of your mental routine. Whether you're facing a tough opponent, a critical audience, or just your own inner critic, remember—you have the tools to face your fears, knock them down, and stride confidently into your next challenge. Let's keep this momentum going!

Today's Goal: Set an egg clock to ring in 15 minutes. Lay down on your back, start by doing 10 breaths with the 4-4-8 technique, then do the Progressive Muscle Relaxation (PMR) technique going through the whole body. Start using the Journal to record every time you have a doom-and-gloom thought. Replace the thought with a positive one and make sure to record that one too. As you have probably understood by now, the end goal is to have NO records in your Journal for days, weeks and months to come.

Day 9: Staying Motivated and Avoiding Burnout

Let's chat about a sneaky little gremlin that can creep up on even the most dedicated athletes — burnout. It's like this annoying background app on your phone that slowly drains your battery without you even noticing. One day, you're firing on all cylinders, and the next, you're wondering why lacing up your sneakers feels like a chore. Understanding the signs of burnout and knowing how to keep your motivation battery charged are crucial for maintaining your sports mojo.

Identifying Burnout: The Warning Signals

So, what does burnout look like? It's not just feeling a bit tired after a tough week; it's a constellation of symptoms that signal you're running low on mental, emotional, and physical energy. Physically, you might feel like you've got a permanent case of the Mondays — tired, drained, maybe even dealing with some nagging injuries that just won't go away. Mentally, it's like your brain has decided to go on a little vacation, leaving you feeling detached, unable to concentrate, and frankly, a bit over it all. Motivation-wise, those goals that used to light a fire in you now barely spark a flicker.

These symptoms can be triggered by repetitive routines, overly intense training without adequate recovery, or the constant pressure to perform at your peak. It's like trying to run a marathon at a sprinter's pace — eventually, something's got to give.

Staying Motivated: Keeping Your Eye on the Prize

Keeping the fire of motivation burning requires a bit of creativity and a lot of self-awareness. First off, mini-goals are your friends. Instead of only focusing on that big, shiny end-of-season trophy, set smaller, achievable targets along the way. Maybe it's improving your time, mastering a new technique, or even just making sure you're having fun at practice. These bite-sized goals can provide a sense of accomplishment and a steady stream of motivation fuel.

Rewards are another great motivator. And no, I'm not just talking about treating yourself to a giant pizza after a game — though that works too! I mean setting up a system where you reward yourself for meeting smaller milestones. Maybe it's a movie night after a week of hitting all your practices, or buying that new gear you've been eyeing after you nail a personal best. These rewards make the journey more enjoyable and remind you that you're making progress, even if it's just one step at a time.

Keeping a positive mindset is like having a good coach inside your head. Surround yourself with positive affirmations, motivational quotes, and reminders of why you love your sport. Listen to inspiring stories of athletes who have overcome challenges. These can serve as mental fuel, reminding you that hurdles are just opportunities for epic jumps.

Preventing Burnout: Balancing Act 101

Now, avoiding burnout isn't just about pushing through; it's about balancing pushing with pausing. Integrating hobbies and social activities outside your sport can be incredibly refreshing. It's like giving your mind and body a mini-vacation — a chance to recharge and return to training with renewed energy and a fresh perspective. Whether it's painting, playing an instrument, or just hanging out with friends, these activities provide a necessary outlet for stress and a reminder that there's more to life than just sports.

Taking mental breaks is equally important. This doesn't mean zoning out in front of the TV; it's about engaging in activities that genuinely relax and rejuvenate your mind. Meditation, yoga, or just some quiet time reading can help clear the mental clutter and reduce the risk of mental fatigue.

Most importantly, listen to your body and mind. They're pretty good at giving you a heads-up when you're pushing too hard. Learn to recognize these signals and adjust accordingly. Maybe it means taking an extra rest day, scaling back on training intensity, or addressing any emotional issues that might be weighing you down.

Incorporating these strategies into your routine doesn't just help you avoid burnout; it makes the entire process of chasing your athletic goals more sustainable and enjoyable. Remember, it's not just about the finish line; it's about enjoying the race. So, keep setting those mini-goals, rewarding your progress, and balancing your life to keep your internal motivation battery-charged and ready to go. Now, let's keep this momentum going and tackle tomorrow with the same vigor and vitality!

The Goal today: Note down in your Journal any early signs of losing your motivation. Also plan and write down smaller achievable targets and what rewards you will give yourself when met.

Day 10: The Role of a Positive Attitude

Ever noticed how a sunny disposition can light up a room, or how a smile from a teammate can make those grueling last minutes of a workout a bit more bearable? That's the power of positivity in action. It's not just about feeling good; it has real impacts on your performance, relationships, and overall well-being. Scientific studies consistently show that a positive attitude can enhance your ability to cope with stress, improve your health, and increase your lifespan. When it comes to sports, the benefits of staying positive can translate into better performance, stronger teamwork, and even faster recovery from injuries. So, how does this all work? Well, positivity helps to broaden your sense of possibility, opens your mind to more options, and enhances your ability to build skills and develop resources.

Cultivating Positivity: Daily Practices

Now, let's talk about cultivating this sunny side, especially on days when the clouds of doubt and defeat loom large. Start with gratitude journaling. This isn't just for the "Dear Diary" moments. It's a powerful tool to shift your focus from what's going wrong to what's going right. Each night, jot down three things you were grateful for that day. Maybe it was a kind word from a coach, a personal best in your training, or simply the opportunity to play the sport you love. This practice trains your brain to start scanning for positives rather than negatives, effectively rewiring your default setting to one that's more optimistic.

Positive self-talk is another game-changer. It's about being the supportive buddy to yourself that you are to others. Notice when you're being self-critical and flip the script. Instead of thinking, "I totally botched that play," try "I'm going to use what I learned in that play to do better next time." It sounds simple, but it makes a huge difference in how you perceive and approach challenges.

Surrounding yourself with positive influences is crucial. This means connecting with teammates who uplift you, coaches who encourage you, and avoiding those energy vampires who may suck the positivity out of you. Your environment plays a huge role in shaping your mindset, so choose your circle wisely, ensuring it's one that fuels your positivity rather than draining it.

Overcoming Negativity: Turning Setbacks into Comebacks

Handling negativity, whether it comes from within or from external sources, is key to maintaining your positive attitude. Start by reframing challenges as opportunities. Got cut from the team? It's a chance to work on your skills and come back stronger. Lost a big game? It's an opportunity to analyze and improve your strategy. This mindset shift doesn't just help you cope with disappointment; it propels you towards future successes.

Another strategy is to learn from setbacks. Instead of stewing in the "what ifs," use these experiences as learning opportunities. Discuss with your coach what you could do differently, seek feedback from teammates, and make a plan for how you can improve. Every setback is a stepping stone to your next victory if you choose to see it that way.

Lastly, keep practicing resilience. This means not giving up when things get tough. Remember, resilience isn't about how you endure, but how you rebound. It's about bouncing back from failures with more knowledge and motivation than before. So next time you face a setback, look it straight in the eye, and say, "Let's dance."

Maintaining a positive attitude isn't about ignoring reality or pretending everything is perfect. It's about choosing to remain optimistic in the face of challenges. It's about seeing the glass as half full, not because you're ignoring how much water is missing, but because you're focused on making the best out of the water you have. Keep nurturing this mindset, and watch as it transforms not just your performance on the field, but your entire life off it. Now, let's carry this positivity forward and tackle what's next with a smile, shall we? Keep shining, keep smiling, and remember, your attitude determines your altitude!

Goal of the day: Start using your Journal each night to write down 3 things you were grateful for that day. Go through the day in your mind and ask yourself if you had any specific opportunities (challenges) to grow. Also, list down all persons that uplift you and do a mental note to connect to them even more from tomorrow and forward.

Day 11: Visualization Techniques

Let's talk about visualization, and no, I'm not referring to daydreaming about your next vacation (though that's fun too). I'm talking about a powerful mental workout that can sharpen your skills, boost your confidence, and enhance your performance without you even breaking a sweat physically. You've already dipped your toes into the basics of visualization in the first week, focusing on seeing your goals and feeling the success. Now, let's dive into the deep end with some advanced techniques that can really turn up the dial on your mental game.

Advanced Visualization: Beyond the Basics

First up, multi-sensory visualization. This isn't just about seeing yourself succeed; it's about engaging all your senses to create a vivid, immersive mental experience. Picture yourself at the starting line of a race. Don't just see the track, hear the crowd, smell the rubber on the hot track, feel the tension in your muscles, and taste the tang of excitement (or your pre-race snack). By engaging all your senses, you make the experience as real as possible, which tricks your brain into thinking you've lived this moment before, making it less daunting when you actually step onto the track.

Now, let's add another layer — scenario planning. This is where you visualize not just the best-case scenario, but also potential challenges. Maybe you stumble at the start in your visualization, or you face unexpected weather. How do you adjust? What do you do? Visualizing overcoming these obstacles prepares you mentally to handle whatever comes your way, ensuring that a hitch isn't the end of your race but just a part of it.

Let me walk you through a guided visualization script. Close your eyes and imagine you're at a crucial game. It's the final play, the score is tied, and the ball is in your hands. Visualize the movement around you, each player's position, the sounds of the game, the feel of the ball, and your planned moves. Now, throw in a twist — another player intercepts. Visualize your response, your recovery, and your adaptability. Feel the determination, the focus, the drive. Open your eyes. How did that feel? Practice this regularly, and watch as these visualized experiences start informing your real responses, making you a more adaptable and confident athlete.

Incorporating Visualization into Training

Integrating visualization into your daily training isn't just beneficial; it's transformative. Start by making it a part of your regular warm-up routine. Just five minutes every day before you start training can set the tone for your session. Visualize the skills you want to focus on that day, the personal bests you aim to beat. This primes your muscle memory and boosts your focus right from the get-go.

Pre-competition visualization is where this tool shines. Before a game or a race, take a moment for a mental run-through. Go through your strategies, visualize dealing with different scenarios, and see yourself succeeding despite them. Athletes who make this a pre-game ritual often find they enter their competitions feeling more prepared, calm, and in control.

The benefits of mental rehearsal are backed by research showing that it can improve motor skills, increase confidence, and reduce competition anxiety. It's like having a rehearsal in a virtual reality setting—completely controlled by you, adaptable, and without the physical strain.

Real-Life Applications: Stories from the Field

Seeing is believing, right? Let's look at some athletes who swear by visualization. Take Michael Phelps, for example. His coach, Bob Bowman, helped him develop a 'videotape' in his mind of the perfect race, which Phelps would 'play' every night before sleep and before each race. This mental rehearsal was so detailed that when Phelps's goggles filled with water during the 2008 Beijing Olympics, he was able to complete the race flawlessly because he had visualized the perfect race so many times—he knew exactly how many strokes he needed to take, even blind.

Then there's Lindsey Vonn, the Olympic skier who uses visualization to not just see but feel every turn and jump of her runs. Before her races, she visualizes the course with such intensity that her muscles twitch, mirroring the movements in her mind. This technique helped her win a gold medal at the 2010 Vancouver Olympics, proving that mental paths can indeed lead to real-life podiums.

These stories aren't just inspiring, they're instructional. They show that whether you're swimming through water, racing down a ski slope, or facing any kind of competitive scenario, the landscape of your mind is just as crucial to conquer as the physical one. So, keep practicing these visualization techniques. Make them as much a part of your training as your physical workouts. The more vividly you can see and feel your success, the more attainable it becomes. Now, let's carry this powerful tool forward and continue building that unstoppable mindset. Keep visualizing, keep training, and keep soaring high!

Goal of the day: Plan and write down your own multi-sensory 'videotape' based on your next upcoming competition or school presentation. Start using 5 minutes of each day and warm up before training sessions to go through your 'videotape.'

Day 12: Building Mental Toughness

Alright, let's talk about mental toughness, a term that's tossed around a lot in sports, but what does it really mean? Imagine you're in the final stretch of a marathon; your legs feel like jelly, and your lungs are burning, but you keep pushing forward. Or you're down by a few points with minutes left on the clock, yet you dial in, focus, and help your team claw back for a win. That's mental toughness. It's that inner grit, resilience, and perseverance that lets you stay focused under pressure, push through exhaustion, and bounce back from setbacks stronger than before.

Mental toughness isn't just about enduring; it's about thriving in the face of challenges. It's what separates good athletes from great ones. It's not just physical endurance but mental stamina. Furthermore, it's your ability to stay focused when the stadium is roaring, to keep cool when the heat is on, and to stay positive when the odds are stacked against you. Embracing challenges, adapting quickly to situations, and seeing setbacks as opportunities to learn and grow are hallmarks of a mentally tough athlete.

Exercises to Develop Mental Toughness

So, how do you build this mental muscle? Just like physical training, it takes consistent work and the right exercises. Let's dive into some practical activities designed to boost your mental toughness:

- **Endurance Drills**: These aren't just for your body; they challenge your mind too. Long runs, extended workouts, or repetitive skill drills push your physical limits and teach you to keep going even when it's tough. The key is to focus not just on the physical execution, but on maintaining a positive mindset throughout. When you think you can't do another lap or another set, that's your mind telling you to quit. Push past it. Learn to talk back to that voice with determination and encouragement.
- **High-Pressure Simulations**: Practice how you play, right? Incorporate scenarios in your training that mimic the pressures of a real game or competition. This could be practicing penalty shots while your teammates shout and distract you, or running drills when you are already fatigued. These simulations help you acclimate to performing under stress, making the actual stressful situations feel more manageable.
- **Mental Endurance Training**: This involves exercises that focus on sustaining concentration and handling stress. Techniques like meditation can enhance your focus, while cognitive-behavioral strategies can help manage stress and anxiety. Regularly practicing these techniques can increase your mental resilience, making you less reactive to stress and more in control of your emotions.

Role Models: Learning from the Mentally Tough

Looking up to athletes who exemplify mental toughness can provide valuable lessons and inspiration. Consider the legendary Muhammad Ali, whose mental game was as fierce as his physical one. His ability to psych out opponents with his confidence and trash talk before a match even started is legendary. Then in the ring, his strategy and endurance under pressure, famously showcased in the "Rumble in the Jungle" against George Foreman, underscore his mental fortitude.

Another great example is Kerri Strug, an Olympic gymnast who performed her final vault with an injured ankle during the 1996 Olympics. Landing on one foot, she clinched the gold medal for her team. Her display of courage and determination under immense physical pain speaks volumes about her mental toughness.

Drawing inspiration from such athletes can motivate you to cultivate your own mental toughness. Study their careers, understand the challenges they faced, and observe how they handled pressure, failure, and success. Integrating these insights with regular mental toughness drills can significantly enhance your ability to handle competitive pressures.

Incorporating these strategies and exercises into your training regimen can transform the way you handle challenges, not just in sports but in all areas of life. Building mental toughness is about strengthening your mind to face and overcome obstacles, to push beyond your limits, and to emerge not just unscathed but victorious. As you continue to train your body, remember to give equal attention to fortifying your mind. After all, the toughest battles are often fought in the arena of the mind.

Today's Goal: See the Netflix movie about the athlete Diana Nyad who sets out at 60 to achieve a nearly impossible lifelong dream: to swim from Cuba to Florida across more than 100 miles of open ocean. Now, that is mental toughness! Get inspired and plan your own endurance drill to do.

Day 13: The Power of Gratitude

Let's chat about gratitude. It's like a secret sauce that can sweeten your life and your performance, both on and off the field. Think of gratitude not just as saying "thanks" but as a powerful mindset that can change the way you look at everything — from your morning run to a grueling practice session. Research has shown that gratitude isn't just polite; it's a booster for mental health, enhancing relationships, and even pumping up your overall happiness. Studies highlight that maintaining an attitude of gratitude can decrease stress, improve sleep quality, and even enhance physical health. It's like giving your mind a giant hug every time you take a moment to appreciate the good stuff, no matter how small.

Daily Gratitude Practice: Turning Thanks into a Habit

Incorporating gratitude into your daily life can be as simple as incorporating a few small practices. Continue with your gratitude journal. This isn't your average "Dear Diary" scenario; it's a tool for transformation. Each day, jot down three things you're thankful for. These could be as simple as a good workout, a helpful coach, or just the chance to compete. The act of writing them down shifts your focus from what's missing or what went wrong to what's abundant and right in your life. It's like resetting your mental GPS from "Stressville" to "Appreciation Lane."

Another fantastic way to weave gratitude into your life is by expressing thanks to others. Make it a point to say thank you to someone every day. Maybe it's your teammate for passing you the ball at just the right moment, or your mom for her endless support. This not only makes the people around you feel good but reinforces your own feelings of gratitude. Plus, it strengthens your relationships, which is pretty much a win-win!

Reflecting on positive experiences each day can also amplify your gratitude. Before you go to sleep, think back on the best moment of your day. Reliving this moment nightly can boost your mood and even help you sleep better. It's like ending your day on a high note, no matter what kind of music life played for you.

Gratitude in Sports: More Than Just a Game

Bringing gratitude into the sports arena can seriously uplift your game. It helps in creating a positive team environment where everyone feels valued and motivated. When teammates express gratitude towards each other, it strengthens bonds and builds a supportive network that can withstand the pressures of competition. It turns the whole team into a more cohesive unit, where everyone is playing not just for themselves, but for each other.

Gratitude also helps keep things in perspective. It's easy to get caught up in the highs and lows of athletic performance—wins can send you soaring, and losses can feel like the end of the world. But a gratitude mindset helps you appreciate the opportunity to compete, to learn, and to grow, regardless of the outcome. It keeps you grounded and focused, not on the scoreboard, but on the deeper value of the sport and your journey within it.

Let's take a leaf out of professional sports, where athletes often use gratitude to enhance their performance. For instance, after a big match, you might see players thanking their coaches, family, and even fans, regardless of the result. They acknowledge that their opportunity to compete at such levels is itself something to be grateful for. This not only endears them to fans but also keeps them mentally healthy and focused. It's about seeing the bigger picture, where every play, every game is part of a larger journey — one that's worth being thankful for.

So, as you lace up your sneakers or tape up your wrists, take a moment to reflect on what parts of your sport and life you're thankful for. Maybe it's the strength in your legs that lets you run, the community of your team, or simply the thrill of the game—whatever it is, let that gratitude fill you up and fuel your practice, your plays, and your interactions. Keep this gratitude practice a part of your daily routine, and watch as it transforms not just your outlook, but your outcomes. Let's keep this positive momentum going, and remember, a thankful heart is a magnet for miracles. Now, let's move forward, ready to tackle tomorrow with gratitude as our guide.

Goal of the day: Say thank you to all family members and one friend at least once during the day. Before you go to sleep, think back on the best moment of your day.

Day 14: Rest and Reflection

Hey, what a ride this week has been, right? Now, let's hit the pause button for a moment. It's time for some good old rest and reflection. Think of this as your halftime break — a chance to huddle up with yourself, assess the plays, and strategize for the next half. It's about taking stock of where you've been, appreciating the progress, and tweaking your game plan as needed. This isn't idle time; it's productive downtime, where real growth happens.

The Importance of Weekly Reflection

Imagine going non-stop, pushing through without ever stopping to check your map. You might end up far off course without even realizing it. That's why regular rest and reflection are crucial. They allow you to see not only how far you've come, but also help clarify where you're heading. Reflection helps consolidate your learning, cementing those skills and strategies you've been working on. It's about connecting the dots between your actions and your outcomes, helping you understand what's working and what's not. Plus, it gives you a moment to breathe, celebrate your efforts, and prepare mentally for the challenges ahead. This isn't just beneficial; it's necessary for sustainable growth and long-term success.

Reflecting after a hectic week might reveal surprising insights. Maybe you notice that you perform better on days when you've had a solid eight hours of sleep, or that your focus sharpens after your morning jog. These nuggets of personal wisdom aren't just interesting tidbits—they're actionable intelligence that can significantly influence your training and performance.

Reflecting on Week 2

So, how about we dive into some reflection? Grab your journal or just a quiet corner and a cup of your favorite drink. Here's what to ponder: What were this week's highs and lows? Maybe you nailed a complex play, or perhaps you struggled with maintaining your motivation. Write it all down. Reflect on why things went the way they did. Was it preparation, mindset, sheer luck, or maybe a mix?

Here are some prompts to get you started:

- What achievement am I most proud of this week?
- What challenges did I face, and how did I handle them?
- What have I learned about myself this week?
- How have my teammates or coaches supported me, and how have I supported them?

This isn't about judging yourself harshly; it's about honest, constructive self-reflection. It's about learning and evolving. Celebrate your progress, no matter how small. Did you push a little harder, stay focused a bit longer, or support your teammates more effectively? Those are wins. Recognize them.

Planning for Week 3

Now, looking forward—what's next? Using the insights from your reflection, start setting your intentions for the upcoming week. This is about proactive planning. What specific areas do you want to focus on? Maybe it's improving your endurance, fine-tuning your technique, or strengthening your mental game. Set clear, achievable goals for these areas.

Consider also how you might adjust your routines or strategies based on what you've learned this week. Maybe you found that you need more downtime between practices, or perhaps a different warm-up routine might better prep you for workouts. Planning isn't just about pushing forward; it's about adjusting the sails to better catch the wind.

Here's a simple framework to guide your planning:

- What are my top three goals for next week?
- What specific steps will I take to achieve these goals?
- Who can support me in reaching these goals, and how will I seek their support?

This proactive approach ensures you're not just drifting along, but are steering actively towards your goals. It's about taking control of your training and your growth, ensuring each week builds on the last, bringing you ever closer to your ultimate objectives.

And just like that, you're ready to jump into next week with a clear plan, a refreshed mind, and a rejuvenated spirit. You've looked back, learned, and looked forward. You're not just moving; you're moving with purpose. Keep this reflective practice a cornerstone of your routine, and watch as it transforms your approach, your mindset, and your outcomes.

Now, as we close this chapter and gear up for the next, carry with you the insights and plans you've crafted. You're building more than just skills; you're building a mindset, a lifestyle, and a future. Next week, we'll dive even deeper, exploring new strategies, facing new challenges, and, as always, growing stronger. Let's do this!

The goal of this day: To use your Journal and reflect on this past week, then plan for next week. Also, Write a review for this Book.

Make a Difference with Your Review

Unlock the Power of Generosity.

Scan the QR code above to leave your review of this book:

"The best way to find yourself is to lose yourself in the service of others." – Mahatma Gandhi

People who give without expecting anything in return live longer, happier lives. So, I'm all in if we can make a difference during our time together.

If you feel good about helping another person, you are my kind of person. Welcome to the club. You're one of us.

If you e-mail a link to your posted review here: review-support@stoneport.se I will send you a 30-Day Journal Template in PDF format to print out and use together with this book to simplify your journaling!

Thank you from the bottom of my heart. Now, back to our regularly scheduled programming.

- Your biggest fan, Mixon Stenhamn

Week 3: Advanced Techniques

Welcome to Week 3, where we crank up the dial on your mental game and dive into some advanced strategies to supercharge your performance. Think of this week as your personal boot camp for the mind, where we toughen up your mental muscles and equip you with ninja-level skills to handle whatever your sport or life throws at you. We're not just playing games here; we're changing the game. Ready to step up? Let's jump right in!

Day 15: Handling Pressure and Expectations

Understanding Pressure: The Invisible Opponent

Pressure, the silent beast lurking in the shadows, ready to pounce when you least expect it. Whether it's the weight of personal expectations, the hopes of your team riding on your shoulders, or the eyes of fans and family watching every move, pressure can squeeze the fun right out of your game if you let it. But here's the kicker: pressure is also a privilege. It means you're in a position to make something amazing happen, to turn all those hours of practice into a performance that leaves a mark.

Let's break down this beast, shall we? First off, there's the pressure you put on yourself. This can be the most intense kind because, let's face it, we're our own toughest critics. Then there's team pressure, where you feel the need to perform not just for yourself, but for your buddies who have been sweating it out alongside you. And don't forget about external pressure from everyone watching — fans, eventual media, even your mom posting every game update on her social media.

Techniques to Manage Pressure: Your Mental Toolkit

Now, how do we keep this beast in check? First up, deep breathing exercises. It sounds simple, but by focusing on your breath, you can dial down the adrenaline and keep panic at bay. Here's a quick guide: breathe in slowly through your nose for four counts, hold it for four, then exhale through your mouth for four. Repeat breathing in this 'triangle' until you feel the tension loosen its grip.

Next, let's talk mindfulness. This isn't just trendy; it's a game-changer. By staying present in the moment, you're less likely to get tangled up in worries about what could go wrong. Practice mindfulness during your routine activities—like tying your shoes or hydrating. Pay attention to the details, the textures, and the sensations, and keep your mind from wandering to the "what ifs."

And then, there's positive self-talk. Replace thoughts like "I can't mess up" with "I'm prepared and ready to shine." It's about coaching yourself and being your own cheerleader. Remember, the conversation you have with yourself is crucial, so make it a supportive one.

Building a Support System: Your Personal Cheer Squad

No one is an island, especially not in sports. Having a solid support system can be your anchor when the pressure feels overwhelming. This includes coaches who guide and motivate, teammates who uplift and support, friends who provide a distraction when needed, and family who provide a safe space to land, win or lose.

Encourage open communication with your support network. Let them know what kind of support you need and when. Maybe it's a pre-game pep talk, or perhaps it's space to process after a tough match. Also, be there for others. Support is a two-way street; being there for your teammates can reinforce your own resilience.

By understanding the sources of pressure and equipping yourself with techniques to manage it, you're setting the stage for performing under pressure, not crumbling under it. And with your personal cheer squad in your corner, you're never alone in the fight. So, take a deep breath, ground yourself in the moment, and get ready to turn pressure into performance. Let's show them what you're made of!

Goal today: List down your 'support network' in your Journal and promise yourself to support them when they need it.

Day 16: Improving Focus with Meditation

Benefits of Meditation: Clearing the Mental Clutter

Imagine your mind as a busy coffee shop. Orders flying in, baristas hustling, a constant buzz of conversation — it's a whirlwind of activity. Now, what if amidst all that chaos, you could find a quiet corner, sit down, and just breathe? That's what meditation can do for you. It's not about emptying your mind or escaping reality; it's about learning to find calm in the chaos and clarity in the clutter. Meditation sharpens your focus, reduces stress, and enhances overall mental clarity, making it a game-changer not just in sports but in every aspect of life.

So, how does meditation work its magic on your brain? When you meditate, you're essentially training your brain to focus and redirect your thoughts. Research shows that regular meditation increases the thickness of the prefrontal cortex, the part of the brain responsible for attention and self-awareness. It's like doing bicep curls but for your brain. Moreover, meditation decreases activity in the default mode network (DMN), the brain network responsible for mind-wandering and self-referential thoughts — often known as the "me center." Lower activity in the DMN means less distraction and more room for focus. Plus, the stress reduction part? That comes from meditation's ability to decrease levels of cortisol, a major stress hormone, which not only helps you feel more relaxed but also improves your ability to handle stress when it does come knocking.

Meditation Techniques: Finding Your Focus Style

Now that you're sold on the wonders of meditation, let's talk about how you can incorporate it into your life. There are several types of meditation, each with its own flavor and benefits, so it's all about finding what works best for you. Let's start with mindfulness meditation, the most widely practiced form. It involves paying attention to your breath as it goes in and out, and observing any bodily sensations, thoughts, or feelings. This type of meditation teaches you to observe without judgment and helps you become more aware of your thoughts and feelings.

Next up is focused attention meditation. This is particularly useful for athletes as it involves focusing on a single point. This could be your breathing, a specific word or phrase (a mantra), or a single point in front of you. It helps improve your ability to concentrate and keeps your mind from wandering.

Then there's the body scan meditation. This involves focusing on different parts of your body and consciously relaxing them. It's a great way to connect with your body, learn where you hold your stress, and physically relax, which can be especially beneficial after a long day of training or competition.

Incorporating Meditation into Your Daily Routine

Let's make meditation as routine as brushing your teeth. The beauty of meditation is that it's incredibly flexible. You don't need any special equipment, and you don't need to spend hours sitting in a lotus position. Just a few minutes a day can make a huge difference. Start by integrating short meditation sessions into your daily routine. Morning is a great time to meditate because it sets a calm, focused tone for your day. Try just five minutes of focused attention meditation when you wake up. Sit in a comfortable position, focus on your breath, and whenever your mind wanders, gently bring your attention back to your breathing.

You can also use meditation during breaks in your day to reset and refocus. A five-minute body scan during your lunch break or between classes or training sessions can help reduce stress and boost your concentration. Lastly, consider a mindfulness session as part of your bedtime routine. It can help calm your mind, reduce stress, and set the stage for a good night's sleep, all of which are crucial for recovery and performance.

By incorporating meditation into your daily life, you're not just improving your focus and reducing stress; you're setting yourself up for better performance in sports and every other area of your life. It's about making meditation a non-negotiable part of your daily training—mental training, that is. So, find your meditation style, weave it into your routine, and watch as your focus sharpens, your stress levels drop, and your performance soars. Now, take a deep breath, and let's continue this mental workout.

Goal of the day: Find a meditation timer app for your phone, download and install it (I use 'Pocket Meditation Timer' found in the App Store for iPhone myself). Set the timer on 5 minutes, do a mindfulness meditation when you wake up and a body scan meditation before going to sleep.

Day 17: Developing Resilience

The Importance of Resilience: Your Comeback Superpower

Hey there, champ! Let's talk about a superpower that every athlete needs, but not everyone talks about enough — resilience. It's what helps you bounce back from those rough games, tough workouts, and unexpected setbacks. Resilience is not about never falling; it's about how quickly and effectively, you can get back on your feet. This mighty skill keeps your spirits up, fuels your motivation, and maintains a positive outlook, no matter the odds. Think of it as your mental immune system, shielding you from the discouragement that can come from setbacks and keeping you focused on your long-term goals.

Resilience in sports is crucial for long-term success. It's what separates those who achieve sustained greatness from those who shine briefly. Every athlete faces challenges — maybe it's a loss in a crucial game, an injury, or just a bad day at practice. Without resilience, these challenges can become insurmountable obstacles. But with it, they transform into stepping stones towards greater achievements. It's about maintaining your cool and keeping your eyes on the prize, even when things don't go as planned.

Building Resilience: Strengthening Your Mental Muscles

So, how do you build this incredible resilience? First, setting **realistic** goals is key. These goals act like checkpoints on your sports journey, helping you navigate through ups and downs. When setting these goals, ensure they're challenging yet achievable — stretch your limits but remain within the bounds of reality. Each small achievement on the way to a bigger goal acts like a resilience booster, reinforcing your belief in your ability to overcome challenges.

Next up is maintaining a growth mindset, which you've already started working on in previous weeks. This mindset is all about seeing challenges as opportunities to learn and grow rather than insurmountable obstacles. When you embrace a growth mindset, you treat setbacks as feedback, not failures. It changes your inner dialogue from "I can't do this" to "I can do this, but not yet." This subtle shift in perspective can significantly increase your resilience, as it keeps you engaged and learning, rather than frustrated and folding.

Practicing self-compassion is another crucial element in building resilience. Be kind to yourself. Understand that no one is perfect, and setbacks are part of the game. Instead of being your own harshest critic, **try to be your own best supporter**. Treat yourself with the same kindness and understanding you'd offer a teammate in a similar situation. This doesn't mean making excuses for poor performances or mistakes, but rather recognizing them as part of your growth process. A practical exercise to enhance self-compassion is to write down a tough situation you faced, how you dealt with it, and one thing you would tell a friend if they were in your shoes. Often, we find that we are much harsher on ourselves than on others.

Real-Life Examples: Resilience in Action

Let's look at some athletes who are the epitome of resilience. Take Derrick Rose, for example. His career has been a roller coaster of high peaks and deep valleys, including being the youngest player to win the NBA MVP and then facing devastating injuries. Each time, he fought his way back into the game, adjusting his play style and continuously working on his physical and mental health. His journey is a powerful testament to resilience, showing that it's possible to rise, fall, and rise again, stronger each time.

Another inspiring story is that of Monica Seles, a former world No. 1 professional tennis player. She faced a traumatic incident when she was stabbed by a spectator during a match. This horrific event could have ended her career, but instead, she took time to recover, both physically and mentally, and returned to tennis to win more titles. Her comeback was a stunning display of mental toughness and resilience, proving that with the right mindset, you can overcome even the most daunting challenges.

These stories highlight that resilience isn't just about bouncing back; it's about bouncing forward, learning from each experience, and coming back stronger. As you incorporate these resilience-building strategies into your life, remember that every setback is a setup for a comeback. Keep pushing, keep learning, and keep growing. Your ability to adapt and overcome is what will define your path in sports and in life. Let's keep this resilience workout going and see just how unstoppable you can become!

Today's Goal: Write down a tough situation you faced, how you dealt with it, and one thing you would tell a friend if they were in your shoes.

Day 18: The Importance of Teamwork and Communication

Let's talk teamwork. Think of the greatest sports teams in history — what made them stand out? It wasn't just the star players or the high-flying dunks and touchdowns. What really set these teams apart was their ability to work seamlessly together, anticipating each other's moves and supporting one another through thick and thin. Effective teamwork can elevate your game, solving problems on the fly, boosting everyone's performance, and skyrocketing motivation. Plus, there's nothing quite like the trust and camaraderie that comes from a team that truly clicks.

Trust is the glue that holds a team together. It's built through shared experiences, reliability, and open communication. When trust is in the mix, players feel secure to take risks, knowing their teammates have their backs. This trust leads to better collaboration, as everyone is more willing to share ideas and strategies without fear of ridicule or rejection. And let's not forget motivation — when you see your teammates giving their all, it's contagious. Suddenly, pushing through that extra mile or tackling that challenging drill doesn't seem so daunting because you're not just doing it for yourself; you're doing it for the team.

Communication Skills: The Game Plan for Success

Now, effective communication is the cornerstone of any successful team. It's about more than just calling plays during a game. It involves active listening, clear articulation, and the ability to give and receive constructive feedback. Sound complicated? Let's break it down with some role-playing exercises that you can try with your team to enhance these skills.

1. **Active Listening Drill**: Pair up with a teammate and discuss a recent game or practice session. One person talks while the other focuses solely on listening — no interruptions, no thinking about how to respond, just pure listening. After summarizing what was said, switch roles. This exercise helps in understanding each other better and ensures that all voices are heard.
2. **Clear Articulation Exercise**: Create a game where each player has to describe a play or strategy without using common sports terms. The others have to guess what is being described. This pushes everyone to communicate more clearly and ensures that the whole team understands what's being discussed, regardless of their level of expertise.
3. **Feedback Circle**: Sit in a circle and have each team member give a piece of constructive feedback to the person on their right, followed by a piece of positive feedback. This should be about recent performances or practices. It's crucial to focus on the behavior or action, not the person, and to be as specific as possible. This can help everyone understand their areas of improvement and strengths, fostering a culture of continuous growth.

WEEK 3: ADVANCED TECHNIQUES

Building Team Cohesion: Crafting a Championship Culture

Creating a positive team environment isn't something that happens overnight. It requires effort and intentionality. Start by setting common goals. These should be clear, achievable, and agreed upon by everyone. Whether it's winning a championship, improving as a unit, or simply supporting each other's personal development, having shared goals can unify the team and provide a clear direction.

Team-building activities can also play a significant role in fostering team cohesion. These don't always have to be sports-related. Something as simple as a team dinner, a group outing, or a team service project can strengthen bonds and build camaraderie. The key is to find activities that allow team members to interact in different settings and build relationships outside the competitive environment.

Lastly, recognize the individual contributions of each team member. Everyone brings something unique to the table, and acknowledging these individual strengths can make each member feel valued and integral to the team's success. This could be through shout-outs at the end of a game, highlighting efforts during team meetings, or even small rewards like the 'player of the week'.

By focusing on effective communication, trust-building, and fostering a supportive team environment, you're not just building a team; you're creating a tight-knit community that can face any challenge together. So, keep these strategies in mind, engage in open dialogues with your teammates, and watch as your collective strength grows, making every practice, every game, and every season more successful and enjoyable.

If CrossFit has its "Workout Of the Day" (WOD) for physical exercise, we could dub the equivalent for psychological exercise as the "Mindset Of the Day" (MOD). It's got a nice ring to it, right? Each day, you'd get a fresh mental challenge or mindfulness practice to keep your brain sharp and your spirit light. Whether it's a mindfulness meditation, a gratitude exercise, or a brain teaser, the MOD could be just the thing to keep your mind in tip-top shape. After all, your brain deserves a good workout too!

Goal Of the Day (MOD from now on): Suggest a team exercise above to your coach, team or family if you are doing a one-man-sport.

Day 19: Handling Setbacks and Failures

You know the drill — life throws a curveball, and suddenly, you're off your game. It happens to everyone, from weekend warriors to seasoned pros. Setbacks and failures aren't just bumps in the road; they're an integral part of the sports landscape. Think of them as harsh tutors with invaluable lessons to share. They test your grit, challenge your resolve, and sharpen your skills. Embracing setbacks as opportunities for growth can transform potential stumbling blocks into stepping stones towards your goals.

Understanding setbacks begins with acknowledging their inevitability. In sports, as in life, not every play goes according to plan. You might miss a crucial shot, fumble a key play, or face a defeat despite your best efforts. These moments can feel like personal failures, but here's the twist — they're not. They are moments of learning, each one packed with insights about your performance, your preparation, and your resilience. The key is to shift your perspective from a fixed mindset, which views setbacks as insurmountable, to a growth mindset, which sees them as opportunities to learn and evolve.

Now, how do you turn these tough moments into growth spurts? Start with reframing failure. This technique involves changing the way you think about and react to setbacks. Instead of seeing a missed goal as a failure, view it as a chance to analyze and improve your shooting technique. It's about finding the lesson in the loss. Here's a practical approach: after a game or performance, take some time to jot down what didn't go as planned. Next to each point, write down what you learned from it and one thing you can do differently next time. This exercise helps in processing the experience and in extracting actionable insights to enhance your future performance.

Seeking feedback is another crucial strategy. It can be tough to hear about your missteps, but constructive criticism is gold in the quest for improvement. Engage with your coach, ask for specifics about what went wrong and what can be improved. If you're a team leader, encourage a culture where feedback is freely exchanged, ensuring it's always given with respect and received with openness. Remember, the goal of feedback is not to point fingers, but to build skills and strategies.

Developing a plan for improvement is your next step. Based on the feedback and your own reflections, outline specific areas for development. Maybe your stamina was lacking, your technique needs tweaking, or your focus waned at a crucial moment. Whatever the gaps, set clear, achievable goals for addressing them. Include specific actions, resources you might need, and a timeline. This plan becomes your roadmap from setback to comeback.

Maintaining a positive attitude throughout this process is crucial. It's easy to stay upbeat when you're winning and everything's going according to plan. The real challenge is keeping your spirits high when the going gets tough. Focus on what you can control — your effort, your attitude, and your actions. Little affirmations can help tremendously. Remind yourself that growth often comes dressed in the garb of failure. Keep handy a few motivational quotes that resonate with you, something like Michael Jordan's famous line: "I've failed over and over and over again in my life, and that is why I succeed."

Celebrating small victories is part of staying positive. Made it through a tough training session? That's a win. Improved your personal best? Celebrate it. These small successes build your confidence back up, reminding you that progress is still being made, even if it's not always in big, dramatic leaps.

Handling setbacks and failures with grace, learning from each experience, and maintaining a positive outlook are not just essential for athletes; they are skills for life. They teach resilience, foster growth, and build character. So the next time you face a setback, take a deep breath, reflect on the lessons, and forge ahead with renewed vigor and clarity. Remember, every champion was once a contender who refused to give up.

MOD: Ask your coach or teammate for specific feedback and develop a plan for improvement today. Identify areas for development like stamina, technique, or focus. Set clear goals, actions, needed resources, and a timeline. At the end of the day, note down what didn't go as planned, what you learned, and one thing to do differently next time. Don't forget to identify and celebrate small victories to build confidence and stay positive during the day.

Day 20: Mental Preparation for Competitions

Pre-Competition Routine: Your Mental Game Plan

Imagine it's the night before the big game. The lights, the crowd, the adrenaline — all waiting for you. But instead of tossing and turning, worrying about the what-ifs, you're cool as a cucumber. Why? Because you've got a killer pre-competition routine that sets you up for success. Think of this routine as your personal pre-game pep talk. It's about getting your head in the game, so your body can follow suit without all the mental clutter.

First off, visualization plays a huge role. By now, you've practiced visualizing your performance in training, but pre-competition visualization is like that final dress rehearsal before the curtain rises. Spend some quiet time envisioning the entire competition, from warming up to playing hard, right through to nailing that win. See yourself executing every move with precision. Feel the success and hear the imaginary crowd roaring. This isn't just daydreaming; it's mentally simulating the event to enhance your real-life performance.

Then there are positive affirmations — your mental armor. These powerful phrases can boost your confidence and calm your nerves. Phrases like "I am prepared," "I am focused," or "I own this field" can reinforce your self-belief and focus your mind on success rather than on potential stumbles. Repeat them like a mantra, especially when doubts try to creep in.

Lastly, don't overlook the importance of relaxation exercises. Techniques such as progressive muscle relaxation, where you tense and then relax different muscle groups, can help release physical tension and mental stress. Even simple deep breathing exercises can center your mind and steady your nerves.

Creating a Pre-Game Ritual: Personalizing Your Prep

Every athlete is unique, which means pre-game rituals can vary wildly. The key is to develop a ritual that resonates with you personally, aligning with your mental and physical preparation needs. Let's take a leaf from the books of some of the most successful athletes. Basketball legend LeBron James, for instance, is known for his pre-game ritual of tossing chalk into the air, a moment that signals his readiness to dominate on the court. It's simple but incredibly symbolic.

Start crafting your own ritual by integrating elements that make you feel prepared and pumped. It could be listening to a specific playlist that gets you in the zone, or maybe it's a series of stretches or warm-up routines that prime your muscles and your mind. It could even be as simple as tying your shoelaces a certain way or wearing a particular accessory that feels like a lucky charm.

Experiment with different activities to see what helps you focus and feel good. The goal is to create a consistent set of actions that help you transition into competition mode. This ritual becomes a signal to your brain and body that it's go-time, helping to elevate your performance when it counts.

Staying Focused During Competition: Keeping Your Head in the Game

Once the game starts, the challenge is to maintain that focus, especially under pressure. This is where mental cues can be incredibly helpful. These short, snappy reminders can bring your focus back if your mind starts to wander mid-competition. Phrases like "focus on the now" or "next move" can anchor you back into the present moment.

Staying present is another crucial aspect. It's easy to get caught up in what just happened — a missed shot, a fumble, or what might happen — will we win, will I score? But the art of staying present, focusing on the current play, the next move, keeps you grounded and in control. Practice mindfulness during your training to strengthen your ability to stay present.

Managing nerves is part and parcel of staying focused. Recognize that it's normal to feel nervous. It means you care about what you're doing. Channel this nervous energy into your performance rather than letting it overwhelm you. Techniques such as breathing exercises can be quick and effective in managing sudden surges of anxiety. Inhale deeply through your nose, hold for a few seconds, and exhale slowly through your mouth. Repeat until you feel more in control.

By creating a solid mental preparation routine, personalizing your pre-game ritual, and using strategies to maintain focus and manage nerves during the competition, you're setting yourself up not just to compete, but to excel. Remember, the body achieves what the mind believes. So gear up, get set, and go conquer that game!

MOD: Create your Pre-Game Ritual that helps you focus and feel good, and

write it down in your Journal sometime during the day. Also, put a rubber band around one of your wrists to remind yourself to be here and now, during the day, focus only on what is in front of you. If you find yourself thinking about anything that happened yesterday or earlier or what is going to happen tomorrow and forward — reward yourself for noticing it and go back to what's in front of you!

Day 21: Rest and Reflection

Ah, the sweet sound of a pause, the quiet moment of stillness — it's not just downtime, it's essential recovery time. As we round off another intense week with the crescendo of advanced techniques, it's crucial to hit the pause button. Why? Because reflection is where the magic of transformation brews. It's your moment to marinate in the experiences, soak up the lessons, and set your sights on new horizons. This isn't just about catching your breath; it's about using that breath to lift you higher.

Rest and reflection might seem like passive activities, but they are anything but that. They are active processes in which you engage deeply with your own experiences, dissecting your actions, emotions, and outcomes. It's about turning the mirror on yourself and really looking — without judgment but with a keen eye for truth. What lessons did this week teach you? How have you pushed your limits? Where did you stumble, and how can you smooth those bumps in the road ahead? This isn't about dwelling on the past; it's about harnessing its power to fuel your future.

Reflecting on Week 3: Celebrate and Contemplate

Let's dive into some reflection prompts that will help you unpack the week. Start by recalling a moment when you felt on top of your game — maybe it was nailing a meditation session or keeping your cool under pressure. What do you think contributed to this success? Was it preparation, focus, or perhaps the supportive cheers of a teammate? Acknowledge and celebrate this — give yourself that well-deserved pat on the back.

Now, pivot to a moment that didn't go as planned. Maybe it was a meditation session that felt more like a mind-racing championship. What pulled your focus away? How did you react emotionally and physically? Identifying these disruptors helps you recognize patterns and plan effective counter-strategies.

Here's a fun exercise: create a two-column list. On one side, jot down what worked this week — actions, strategies, and mindsets that drove you forward. On the other, note what didn't work. For each point in the second column, brainstorm a potential solution or adjustment. This exercise not only clarifies your path forward but actively engages you in the problem-solving process, making you a proactive player in your own development.

Planning for Week 4: Setting the Stage for Success

With insights in hand from your reflection, let's look ahead. The final week looms large, filled with opportunities to apply what you've learned and to stretch even further. Start by reviewing your routines and strategies. What needs a tweak? Maybe it's adding an extra five minutes to your meditation practice or adjusting your pre-game affirmations to better address the nerves.

Set some intentions for the upcoming week. These should be specific and aligned with the areas you've identified as needing improvement. Perhaps you aim to enhance your focus during high-pressure moments or to support a teammate who's struggling. Whatever your intentions, write them down. Make them real. This act of writing commits you to your goals and serves as a tangible reminder of your game plan.

Lastly, mentally prepare for the challenges ahead. Visualize yourself tackling the week with gusto, using your newly honed skills to navigate whatever comes your way. Imagine the satisfaction of hitting new personal bests, the joy of deeper connections with teammates, and the pride of knowing you gave it your all.

As you wrap up today's reflection and planning, remember that this process is about growth. Each reflection deepens your understanding, and each plan sets the stage for your next victory — on and off the field. Carry forward the momentum you've built, the lessons you've learned, and the resilience you've fortified. The upcoming week is just another chance to shine brighter, push further, and climb higher.

As we close this week and look towards the final leg of our journey together, take a moment to appreciate how far you've come. The strides you've made are not just about better performance, but about building a better you. Next week, we bring all these threads together, weaving them into a comprehensive strategy that's not just about sports but about life. Ready? Let's make this next week legendary.

MOD: Create the two-column list in your Journal. Write down what worked this week on one side, and what didn't work on the other. Brainstorm a potential solution or adjustment for each point in the second column. Then review your routines and strategies. What needs a tweak? Set some intentions for the upcoming week. Lastly, mentally prepare for the challenges ahead by visualizing yourself tackling the week heads on, using your new skills to navigate whatever comes your way. Imagine the satisfaction of new personal bests, the joy of deeper friendship with teammates, and the knowledge that you gave it your all.

Week 4: The Final Push

Welcome to the final stretch, team! Think of this week as the last quarter of a tightly contested game, the final act of an epic movie, or that heart-pounding last mile of a marathon. It's where everything you've learned, practiced, and experienced coalesces into pure performance magic. This week, we're not just crossing the finish line; we're breaching new frontiers of mental toughness and capability. So, lace up those sneakers, flex those neurons, and let's show the world what you're made of!

Day 22: Integrating Mindfulness into Daily Life

Understanding Mindfulness: More Than Just a Buzzword

Mindfulness might sound like a serene, slightly mystical practice reserved for yogis and meditation gurus, but don't be fooled — it's as practical and down-to-earth as the sweat on your gym shorts. At its core, mindfulness is about being fully present in the moment. For athletes like you, this could mean feeling the turf under your feet, listening to the rhythmic thump of your heart during a sprint, or noticing the grip of your fingers on a basketball. It's about tuning into the now, with all its sensations and nuances, which can dramatically improve focus, reduce stress, and enhance overall performance.

The benefits are backed by science, too. Studies have shown that mindfulness can decrease cortisol levels — the stress hormone — improve attention span, and even enhance immune function. Imagine being able to lower your stress levels before a big game or recover faster because your immune system is in tip-top shape. That's the power of mindfulness at your fingertips.

Practical Applications: Mindfulness Made Easy

Integrating mindfulness into your daily routine doesn't require sitting cross-legged for hours — unless that's your thing, of course. It's about finding small, practical ways to be more present throughout your day. Let's start with something you already do every day: eating. Mindful eating involves paying full attention to the experience of eating and drinking. It's about noticing the colors, smells, textures, and flavors of your food, chewing slowly, and savoring each bite. This practice can help improve your digestion and even enhance your satisfaction with your meals.

Next, let's talk about mindful breathing. This can be a game-changer in high-pressure situations. Again, try the "Box Breathing" technique: breathe in for four counts, hold for four counts, exhale for four counts, and hold again for four counts. It's like hitting the reset button on your nervous system, bringing you back to a state of calm and control.

Mindful listening is another great tool, especially useful in team sports. It involves fully concentrating on the sounds around you, whether it's the coach's instructions, teammates' calls, or even the crowd's reactions. This can enhance your situational awareness and reaction time on the field or court.

Daily Mindfulness Practice: A Routine That Sticks

To make mindfulness a staple in your daily regimen, consider setting aside specific times for brief mindfulness exercises. It could be a few minutes of mindful breathing every morning when you wake up or a quick session of mindful observation, where you pause to visually absorb everything around you, before practice. The key is consistency. The more you practice mindfulness, the more natural it will become, and soon, you'll find yourself being mindful without even having to think about it.

Consider incorporating mindfulness prompts into your environment. A sticky note on your locker that says, "Pause, Breathe, Focus" can serve as a quick reminder to center yourself during the day. Apps that send you mindful reminders or guided meditations can also be incredibly useful tools in your mindfulness journey.

By weaving mindfulness into the fabric of your daily life, you're not just enhancing your performance in sports; you're building a skill that will serve you well in every aspect of your life. Whether you're facing a high-stress exam, a crucial meeting, or a personal challenge, mindfulness gives you the power to stay calm, focused, and overwhelmingly positive. So, embrace these final days of training with open arms and a mindful heart, and prepare to be amazed at how far you've come and how much further you can go.

MOD: Take a large piece of paper, write down 'MEDITATE for 5 MIN' in large, bold letters, and place it on the roof just above you when you are lying down on your bed with your head on the pillow. This way, you will be reminded to do just that every morning when waking up and every evening before going to sleep. Also, practice mindful eating today — yes, that means for all today's meals: breakfast, lunch and dinner. That goes for any snacks or anything else between your meals as well.

Day 23: The Role of Mentors and Role Models

Finding Inspiration: Your Guiding Stars in Sports and Life

Think of your sports career as a vast ocean you're navigating. Now, imagine having seasoned captains aboard your ship, guiding you through rough waters and pointing out the best routes. That's what mentors and role models do in your athletic and personal development voyage— they steer you clear of common pitfalls and inspire you to push beyond your limits.

Having a mentor or role model in sports isn't just about emulating someone else's success; it's about having a tangible example of what's possible when you mix talent with relentless dedication. They are living proof that your goals are attainable, providing not just inspiration but also practical strategies and moral support along your path. Whether it's a coach who has always believed in your potential even when you didn't, a senior athlete who has navigated the challenges you face, or even a professional player whose career you follow closely, each of these figures adds a layer of enrichment to your sports journey.

These guiding stars do more than just lead the way; they also light a fire under you when your motivation is a flickering flame. They remind you why you started when the grind gets tough and the glamour fades. They show you that every training session, every game, and every setback is a stitch in the fabric of a greater narrative of success. This is crucial in moments of doubt, making the role of mentors and role models indispensable in the world of sports.

Identifying Mentors: Building Your Support Network

Finding the right mentor can feel a bit like dating — you need to find someone whose experiences, values, and skills align with your aspirations. But where do you start? Look around you; potential mentors are often closer than you think. It could be a coach, a teacher, or even a family member who has always championed your dreams. These individuals should possess qualities that resonate with you: resilience, wisdom, empathy, and a genuine interest in helping others succeed.

Approaching potential mentors can be intimidating, but remember, most people are flattered to be asked for guidance. Start by expressing genuine interest in their career and experiences. Ask insightful questions that go beyond surface-level inquiries. For example, instead of just asking about their successes, dive into the lessons they've learned from failures or the strategies they've found most effective in overcoming challenges.

Once you've established a connection, be clear about what you're seeking from the mentorship. Are you looking for advice on specific skills, strategic career guidance, or moral support? Being upfront about your needs and expectations helps set the tone for a productive relationship. Most importantly, show commitment. Be proactive in seeking advice, punctual in your interactions, and gracious for your time and insights. Mentorship is a two-way street; your engagement and appreciation for their time are key.

Learning from Role Models: Absorbing Success Patterns

Role models might not be mentors with whom you interact directly, but they can still have a profound impact on your development. Choose role models whose paths or qualities you admire and study them. This doesn't mean blindly copying their choices. Instead, analyze the principles behind their actions and the habits that contribute to their success.

For instance, if your role model is a renowned basketball player, look beyond their scoring stats. Study their work ethic, how they handle press interviews, how they recover from injuries, and how they contribute to their team's dynamics. Each of these aspects offers lessons on professionalism, resilience, and teamwork.

Keep a notebook where you jot down qualities or habits you observe in your role models that you wish to develop. Reflect on these notes regularly and assess how you can integrate these aspects into your own training and competitions. Remember, the goal isn't to become a carbon copy of your role model but to be inspired by them to forge your own path of excellence.

By embracing the influence of mentors and role models, you equip yourself with a compass and map for your sports career. You gain access to wisdom earned through experience, motivational boosts during tough times, and practical strategies that pave the way to your goals. As you push forward in your final week of mental toughness training, keep the lessons and inspirations from your mentors and role models close. They are not just guides; they are part of your team, your cheerleaders, and at times, your navigators, helping you chart a course to success that is uniquely yours.

MOD: Write down what you want to get out of a mentorship, guess where… yes — in your Journal. Also, put down qualities or habits of your role models that you wish to develop yourself. Then identify potential mentors in your neighborhood that could give you all or parts of what you need. If they also have some of the role model qualities and habits you admire — that's icing on the cake.

Day 24: Fine-Tuning Your Routine

Assessing Your Routine: Is It Working for You?

Imagine your daily routine as your personal sports playbook. Just like any savvy coach, you need to review and tweak it regularly to ensure it's setting you up for those big wins, not just in sports, but in life too. Let's kick off with a solid self-assessment. Grab your notebook and let's get analytical. List down everything that's currently part of your daily grind. Yes, everything—from the moment your alarm buzzes you awake to the minute you hit the pillow. Now, next to each activity, jot down two things: how much energy this activity requires and how much joy it brings you. It's like measuring each part of your day on a "cost-benefit" scale.

Next up, identify the mismatches. Are there high-energy tasks that just don't seem to pay back much in terms of satisfaction or results? Maybe it's that extra hour of mindless scrolling through social media, or perhaps the elaborate lunch prep that leaves you more frazzled than fulfilled. These are your potential cutbacks. Conversely, spotlight the activities that score low on effort but high on rewards. Maybe a quick morning meditation leaves you surprisingly serene, or a brief afternoon walk recharges your batteries beyond expectation. These are your keepers.

Here's a pro tip: create a visual representation of your day—a pie chart, perhaps—to give you a clear overview of how your time is being spent. This can be a real eye-opener, revealing how much time you're actually dedicating to productive activities versus energy drainers. Armed with this knowledge, you're ready to tweak your routine not just to survive your day, but to conquer it.

Making Adjustments: Keeping It Flexible

Now that you've dissected your routine, it's time to play mad scientist and experiment a bit. The goal here is flexibility—creating a routine that bends without breaking, especially when life throws those inevitable curveballs. Start by prioritizing. What's non-negotiable? For most athletes, training and recovery time are sacred. But what about the other pieces? This is where you get to shuffle things around based on your current goals and demands.

Think of your energy levels as a battery that needs to be managed wisely throughout the day. Place the most demanding tasks at your peak energy times. Not a morning person? Maybe save that intense workout for late afternoon when you're fully revved up. Then, slot in your less demanding tasks during your energy lulls. This kind of strategic planning can transform an average day into an optimized performance showcase.

But here's the kicker — life is unpredictable. Maybe rain cancels practice, or an unexpected project lands on your desk. This is where your newfound flexibility becomes your superpower. Have backup plans ready. Maybe swap a rained-out practice for a gym session or a yoga class. The more adaptable your routine, the less stress you'll feel when changes occur, and the more fluidly you'll navigate your day.

Personalizing Your Routine: Make It Uniquely Yours

Your routine should be as unique as your fingerprint, perfectly tailored to your life's rhythms, challenges, and joys. Start by understanding your body's natural clock. Are you a night owl or an early bird? Align your routine to capitalize on the times when you feel most energetic. Next, factor in your personal and professional commitments. A student-athletes's routine looks very different from that of a professional entering their off-season.

Don't forget to inject elements that boost your mental and emotional well-being. Maybe it's listening to your favorite podcast while you stretch, or winding down with a chapter of a good book at night. These personal touches can make the difference between a routine that feels like a straitjacket and one that feels like a tailored suit.

And here's something fun — why not borrow ideas from athletes in other sports? A basketball player might benefit from the disciplined sleep routines often adhered to by swimmers, or a football quarterback might find value in the visualization techniques used by gymnasts. Experimenting with these cross-disciplinary strategies can freshen up your routine and introduce you to benefits you might never have considered.

In essence, fine-tuning your routine isn't just about shuffling tasks around—it's about crafting a daily flow that supports your goals, respects your energy levels, and satisfies your soul. It's about living intentionally, not just reactively. So, as you continue to refine your routine, remember that each day is a fresh chance to live better, perform better, and be better. Here's to making each day, each action, and each moment count!

MOD: List down everything that's currently part of your daily grind in the Journal. Next to each activity, put down two things: how much energy this activity requires and how much joy it brings you. Next, identify the mismatches. Cut back on the daily activities that consume much time and

energy but give low value in return. Keep the other activities on your daily schedule and even increase the effort on those. Place the most demanding activities at your peak hours.

Day 25: Reflecting on Your Journey

The Power of Reflection: Seeing the Big Picture

Let's talk about reflection — not the kind you see in a mirror, but the kind that involves looking back at your experiences to gather insights and pave the way for future triumphs. Think of reflection as your mental replay system, allowing you to revisit past performances, decisions, and strategies, not just to relive them, but to learn from them. This practice is like having a superpower that boosts personal growth and self-awareness, helping you spot patterns, celebrate successes, and pinpoint areas ripe for improvement.

Reflecting regularly offers you a panoramic view of your progress and challenges. It's like stepping back to look at a mosaic — each piece might be interesting on its own, but stepping back to see the whole picture can be truly enlightening. This broad perspective can help you understand how individual actions contribute to long-term outcomes, and how even small adjustments can lead to significant improvements. Moreover, this practice can solidify your identity as an athlete and a learner, reinforcing both your strengths and your commitment to continuous growth.

Reflection Exercises: Digging Deeper

Diving into reflection can be as simple or as structured as you need it to be, but here's a way to structure this process to make the most out of it. Start with setting aside a quiet time at the end of each day or week — think of it as an appointment with yourself. Grab a journal and write down key events: the highs, the lows, and the unexpected turns. But let's go deeper than just stating what happened. Reflect on three crucial aspects:

1. **Successes**: What were your wins? These could be anything from nailing a complex play, achieving a new personal best, or simply maintaining consistency in your training. Describe what these successes felt like and what they taught you.
2. **Challenges**: What obstacles did you face? More importantly, how did you respond to them? Did you tackle them head-on, or was there hesitation? Analyze what these challenges could be signaling. Maybe they're areas for skill development, or perhaps they're pointing toward the need for a strategy tweak.
3. **Key Learnings**: From everything you've written down, what are the major takeaways? Perhaps you've learned something about your emotional triggers or discovered a new technique that improves your focus.

These reflection prompts not only guide you through a thorough analysis of your past experiences but also transform these insights into actionable knowledge. Engaging regularly in this exercise can fine-tune your approach to training and competition, ensuring that each step you take is informed by a well-considered review of your past actions.

Learning from Experience: Crafting Your Future Playbook

Harnessing the power of your reflections is where the real game begins. Each insight you gather is like a piece of gold, valuable and transformative. Begin by using these reflections to inform your future actions. If you noticed, for instance, that your performance peaks during morning training sessions, could you rearrange your routine to capitalize on that? Or, if you found that certain strategies consistently lead to success, how can you integrate these more deeply into your game plan?

Take these reflections and turn them into a blueprint for your ongoing training and competitions. Set up experiments based on your learnings. Maybe you tweak your warm-up routine or try a new mental visualization before games. Monitor the outcomes of these adjustments closely. Are they bringing you closer to your goals? Are they improving your performance? This methodical application of insights ensures that you are not just moving forward, but moving forward in a way that is aligned with your personal growth and performance goals.

Moreover, sharing these insights can be incredibly beneficial. Discuss your reflections with coaches, mentors, or teammates. They can offer new perspectives or advice that might help you refine your approach even further. This collaborative reflection not only enhances your own understanding but can also foster a deeper sense of team cohesion and mutual growth.

As you continue pushing forward, remember that reflection isn't just about looking back—it's a dynamic tool that propels you forward, informed, and ready to tackle whatever comes next. So, keep this reflective dialogue with yourself alive. It's one of the most effective ways to ensure that every step you take is thoughtful, informed, and poised for success.

MOD: Book a quiet time at the end of the day or week. Grab your journal and write down key events: the highs, the lows, and the unexpected turns. Then ask yourself: 1) Successes: Your wins? What did they feel like? What did they teach you? 2) Challenges: What obstacles did you meet? How did you respond to them? Did you tackle them head-on, or did you hesitate? What could these challenges be signaling? Are there areas for the development of skills? Are there signs of a need for strategy tweaks? 3) Key Learnings: Are there any major takeaways?

Day 26: Maintaining Your Momentum

Sustaining Progress: Keeping the Wheels Rolling

Alright, you've been pushing hard, nailing your daily routines, and crushing those mental challenges. But as we hit Day 26, the real question isn't just how you keep the momentum going for the next few days, but how you keep this energy burning long after these 30 days are a wrap. Think of momentum like a snowball rolling down a hill — the more it rolls, the bigger and faster it gets. Your job? Keep that snowball rolling, no matter what the terrain looks like.

First up, let's talk about setting new goals. It's like plotting points on your GPS after you've reached your initial destination. There's always more to explore, right? Setting new goals keeps you moving forward, avoiding that post-challenge slump that can sneak up like a ghost if you're not careful. These don't have to be monumental goals. Sometimes, the smaller, more immediate goals can pack the most punch. Aim to improve a technique, shave a few seconds off your run, or master a new strategy in your playbook. The key is to keep setting these markers for yourself, keeping your journey dynamic and your spirits high.

Consistency in your routines is your secret weapon here. It's the rhythm to your blues, the heartbeat to your song — it keeps everything flowing. Whether it's the daily workouts, the mental conditioning, or the healthy eating, each piece plays a vital role in maintaining your momentum. It might feel tempting to take a breather once you hit a big milestone, but remember, top performers know that consistency is the glue that holds progress together. It's what turns 'one-time' into 'all-the-time'.

And don't forget to continue your mental training. It's easy to focus on physical stamina and strength, but your mental muscles need just as much attention to keep you at the top of your game. Keep challenging yourself with mental exercises, keep your focus sharp with mindfulness practices, and keep your motivation burning with positive affirmations. These tools aren't just for the 30-day challenge; they're for your everyday lifelong challenge!

Dealing with Plateaus: Climbing the Invisible Hills

Even the best of us hit plateaus — those sneaky stretches where progress seems to stall, motivation wanes, and everything feels a bit more like a grind. It's like you're running as hard as you can, but the scenery's just not changing.

Frustrating, right? But here's the thing about plateaus: they're not just obstacles; they're opportunities — invitations, really — to mix things up and reignite your momentum.

First, recognize the plateau. Keep an eye on your performance metrics and personal feelings. Feeling stuck? Seeing less improvement? You're likely on a plateau. Now, instead of letting frustration set in, get curious. What's working? What's not? Sometimes, all it takes is a small tweak in your routine or strategy to jumpstart your progress. Maybe it's adjusting your training intensity, trying a new technique, or even seeking feedback from a coach or mentor.

Staying motivated through these periods is crucial. Set mini-challenges for yourself, celebrate small victories along the way, and remind yourself of your why — why you started, why you're pushing, and why you're committed to this path. These reminders can be powerful motivators, turning a slog through the mud into a dance in the rain.

Long-Term Commitment: Building a Legacy of Growth

This isn't just about being good for a season or even a year. It's about building a legacy of growth that spans your entire career and life. Think about athletes who've sustained success over the long haul — they all share a commitment not just to the sport but to continuous improvement and adaptation. They evolve as the game evolves, they learn from new challenges, and they stay committed through ups and downs.

Embrace this long-term vision for yourself. Envision where you want to be in five, ten, or even twenty years. What kind of athlete do you want to be? What kind of person? Hold these visions close; let them guide your daily choices and efforts. And remember, commitment isn't just about sticking with the good times; it's about pushing through when the going gets tough, when the glamour fades, and the crowds quiet down. That's when your true commitment shines.

Continually seek new learning opportunities, stay adaptable, and keep pushing your boundaries. Whether it's learning from younger athletes, embracing new training technologies, or adapting to new rules and styles in your sport, staying open and adaptable ensures you keep growing, no matter how much the game changes.

So, as you gear up each day, remember that maintaining your momentum isn't just about keeping pace, it's about setting the pace, pushing the boundaries, and leaving a trail of growth in your wake. Let's keep this energy alive, let's keep striving for greatness, and let's make sure that every day is an opportunity to be better than yesterday.

MOD: Think of the last time you were on a plateau, or are you in one now? Note down in your notebook how you recognize(d) it as a plateau. How did you or do you feel? What did you or do you see? Note it down so you can recognize it even faster next time it happens.

Day 27: Setting Future Goals

Today, let's grab the steering wheel of your athletic destiny and navigate through the maze of goal setting with a fresh set of eyes. Think of today as a day of recalibration, where we look back at the targets we hit (or missed), and then chart a path forward with new milestones. It's like updating your game's level when you know you've got the skills to tackle bigger challenges. But hey, we're not just throwing darts in the dark here; we're methodically carving out steps towards a future where you stand taller, run faster, and hit harder, all with a grin of satisfaction that comes from smashing your personal bests.

Evaluating Goals: The Rearview Mirror

First up, let's perform a little time travel back to Day 1. Remember those goals you set? Let's pull them up — every single one of them. This isn't just about ticking boxes; it's about understanding the 'why's' behind the checks and the crosses. For each goal, ask yourself: Did I achieve this? If yes, what worked in my favor? Was it the extra hours of training, the adjusted diet, or perhaps the mental conditioning exercises? Understanding the recipe for your success is crucial because, let's face it, you're going to want to whip up that dish of success again and again.

Now, for the goals you didn't meet — let's not call them failures; let's call them 'not yets'. Analyze what held you back. Was the goal too ambitious? Did unforeseen obstacles throw you off track? Or did your motivation wane? This reflection isn't about beating yourself up. It's about arming yourself with knowledge for better goal-setting in the future. It's learning that maybe setting a marathon goal during your finals week wasn't the best timing, or that aiming to cut down three seconds on your lap time in one week was a tad ambitious.

SMART Goals Revisited: Sharpening Your Tools

Ah, SMART goals—our old friends. Specific, Measurable, Achievable, Relevant, and Time-bound. Sounds familiar, right? But let's not just breeze through these like a checklist. Let's dive deep. Your goals need to be as sharp as the skates on a hockey player at the Stanley Cup finals. Specificity is your friend. Instead of saying, "I want to get better at basketball," zone in on what 'better' means. Does it mean improving your shooting accuracy, enhancing your dribbling skills, or perhaps mastering the art of rebounds?

Make it measurable. Put numbers on it so you can clearly see whether you've hit it or not. Achievable is about being honest with yourself — stretch your limits but recognize your current limits. Relevant ensures your goals align with your bigger ambitions. Why waste time perfecting a backstroke if you're aiming to be a sprinter? And finally, time-bound — every goal needs a finish line. Whether it's three weeks or six months, set a date. It's your 'when'.

Creating an Action Plan: Your Roadmap to Victory

With your shiny new or tweaked SMART goals, it's time to build the bridge that will lead you to them. This starts with an action plan that breaks each goal into bite-sized steps. Think of it as creating a mini-roadmap for each goal. If your target is to enhance your free-throw accuracy, your action plan might include specific drills, scheduled practice times, and weekly progress evaluations.

Tracking your progress is crucial. Whether it's a training log, a digital tracker, or a good old-fashioned journal, keeping a record helps you stay on course and make adjustments as needed. It also serves as a motivational booster; nothing beats seeing your own progress in black and white.

And let's talk about accountability. Sometimes, the journey can get lonely. Find a training buddy, hire a coach, or join a community. When you share your goals with someone else, they help keep you accountable. Plus, it's always more fun to celebrate those victories with someone who's been in the trenches with you.

As you set these new goals and chart out your plans, remember, this process is dynamic. Life changes, circumstances shift, and your goals might need to adapt. Stay flexible, but keep your eyes on the prize. With every meticulously set goal and carefully crafted action plan, you're not just dreaming of a future—you're actively building it, one achievement at a time. So, let's get to it, and may your aim be as true as an archer's arrow and your resolve as steadfast as a marathoner's stride.

MOD: Pull the goals from Day 1 up. For each goal, ask yourself: Did I achieve

this? If yes, what worked in my favor? If no, why not? Now, delete them, change them, create new SMART goals based on your analysis. For each goal, create an action plan with specific drills, scheduled practice times and weekly evaluations. Share your reworked and new goals with someone that can hold you accountable.

Day 28: Visualization and Relaxation

Advanced Visualization: Crafting Your Inner Cinema

Picture this: you're not just going through the motions in your mind, you're directing a blockbuster where you're the hero, nailing every play, overcoming every obstacle, and achieving every goal with cinematic flair. That's the essence of advanced visualization, a technique that goes beyond simple mental rehearsals. It involves immersing yourself in complex, dynamic scenarios, engaging all your senses to create a vivid, multi-dimensional experience. This isn't just visualization; it's a full-on mental simulation.

Imagine you're facing a particularly challenging opponent next week. Instead of just picturing a generic victory, visualize the entire scene in detail. Feel the texture of the ball, hear the crowd, see the opponent's jersey flutter as they move, smell the fresh-cut grass, and taste the tang of your sports drink at halftime. Walk yourself through specific game strategies you plan to use, visualize adapting to unexpected plays, and see yourself triumphing over challenges with grace and strategy. This kind of detailed visualization prepares you mentally to handle real-game pressures and pivot as needed, making you not just a participant in your sports narrative, but the master of it.

To enhance this practice, incorporate emotional responses. How will you feel after making a crucial block or scoring the decisive point? Let those feelings of accomplishment, joy, and pride wash over you in your visualization. These emotional rehearsals boost your psychological readiness, reinforcing your belief in your ability to succeed. It's like giving your brain a preview, a taste of victory, so when the moment comes, your mind and body already know the drill.

Relaxation Techniques: Unwinding the Champion Within

Now, let's shift gears and talk about unwinding. Yes, even the most relentless warriors need to sheathe their swords and rest. Relaxation techniques are crucial for balancing the mental and physical stresses of training and competition. Progressive muscle relaxation (PMR) is a fantastic method to release tension not just from the body, but also from the mind. It involves tensing each muscle group in your body for a few seconds, then releasing the tension, allowing a wave of relaxation to wash over each part. Start from your toes and work your way up to your forehead. It's not just relaxing; it's a way to get in tune with your body and recognize areas where you might be holding stress without even realizing it.

Deep breathing exercises are another cornerstone of a solid relaxation routine. Try the 4-7-8 technique: breathe in deeply for four seconds, hold the breath for seven seconds, and exhale slowly for eight seconds. This method helps reduce anxiety, slows down a racing heart, and brings clarity to your mind — a perfect way to center yourself after a high-octane day or to calm pre-game jitters.

Guided imagery, where you visualize a peaceful and relaxing scene — like a quiet beach at sunset or a serene path through a forest — can also be a powerful tool. This technique not only relaxes the mind but also rejuvenates it, preparing you for the next round of challenges. Consider integrating audio recordings of guided imagery that detail these calming scenarios, enhancing the experience and making relaxation an easily accessible refuge.

Integrating into Training: Weaving Calm Through the Chaos

Incorporating visualization and relaxation techniques into your regular training and competition prep isn't just beneficial; it's a game-changer. Start with making these practices a routine part of your pre-game preparations. Just as you might strategize game plays or warm up physically, dedicate time for mental warm-ups using visualization. Picture the upcoming game, imagine handling various scenarios, and see yourself performing optimally. This mental prep sets a positive, confident tone for the game.

Relaxation techniques can be woven into your post-game routines as well. After the adrenaline fades and the crowd's roar dims, engage in PMR or deep breathing exercises to bring your body back to a state of calm and prevent the build-up of residual stress. These practices not only enhance your recovery but also improve your sleep quality, ensuring you're rested and ready for whatever the next day throws at you.

Incorporating these techniques into your training isn't just about improving your physical performance; it's about cultivating a resilient, focused, and calm mind. The ability to visualize success and relax deeply is as much a part of your athletic arsenal as your physical skills. So, embrace these practices with the same enthusiasm as a physical workout. After all, a calm mind is the ultimate weapon against the chaos of competition.

MOD: Incorporate one blockbuster visualization and one favorite relaxation technique into your regular training and competition. Yes, you should write these down, too.

Day 30: Celebrating Your Achievements

Acknowledging Progress: The Fuel for Your Fire

Hey there, champions! Here we are, at the grand finale of our 30-day crash course in mental toughness and peak performance. You've pushed through limits and danced out of your comfort zones, and now, it's time to hit the pause button — not to stop, but to celebrate. Yes, every sprint, every leap, and every challenge you've taken head-on deserves a moment of recognition. Celebrating isn't just about giving yourself a pat on the back; it's about fueling your journey forward. It boosts your motivation, lifts your spirits, and solidifies the gains you've made, both big and small.

Think of your achievements as milestones on a marathon route. Each one you pass is a tangible reminder of how far you've come and a burst of energy to keep you running. Celebrating these moments can transform your perception of your journey from a grueling slog to an exhilarating adventure. It's about shifting focus from what's next to what's now, and giving yourself the credit you richly deserve. Whether it's nailing a complex move, improving your personal best, or simply sticking to your training on days when you want to quit, each accomplishment is a stepping stone to greater heights.

But here's the kicker — acknowledgment isn't just for the big, shiny successes. It's also for the small, gritty ones that no one sees. It's for those mornings you got out of bed to train when the sun hadn't even peeked over the horizon. It's for choosing a salad over fries when every fiber of your being screams for comfort food. These victories are just as worthy, if not more because they lay the groundwork for the bigger triumphs.

Celebration Ideas: Making It Memorable

Now, how do you celebrate in a way that's meaningful and memorable? It doesn't always have to be about throwing a party (though who doesn't love a good celebration?). It can be as simple or as grand as you like. How about hosting a small dinner with your teammates or training buddies? Share stories from your training, laugh over the bloopers and cheer for each other's victories. It's a great way to strengthen bonds and build team spirit.

Or perhaps treat yourself to something special. Maybe it's that new gear you've been eyeing, a day at the spa to soothe those worked muscles, or simply an afternoon off with your favorite book or video game. The key is to do something that feels rewarding and aligns with the hard work you've put in.

Sharing your success can also amplify your joy. Post your achievements on social media, write a blog post, or just call your family. Letting others in on your triumphs allows them to celebrate with you, and their words of encouragement can be an incredible boost.

Looking Ahead: Carrying the Torch Forward

As we wrap up this intense, rewarding month, it's crucial to look forward. The end of this 30-day challenge is really just the beginning. The habits you've formed, the skills you've honed, and the mental toughness you've cultivated are now integral parts of your arsenal. They are tools that will serve you well beyond the realms of sports. Whether it's tackling a tough project at work, managing stress in your personal life, or taking on new hobbies, the resilience and focus you've developed here are yours to command in every arena of life.

So, what's next on your horizon? Set new goals, perhaps even more ambitious than before. Challenge yourself to push the boundaries of what you believe is possible. Remember, growth doesn't have an endpoint; it's a continuous journey. Each goal you set and meet is not just an achievement; it's a launchpad for the next challenge, the next adventure.

Let the momentum you've built propel you into future endeavors with confidence and gusto. Keep the routines that work for you, tweak what needs improvement, and always keep your sights set on new heights. The discipline, determination, and resilience you've embraced over these past 30 days are more than just traits; they're your companions on a lifelong journey toward excellence.

And there you have it — 30 days of pushing limits, shattering barriers, and setting the stage for continued success. As you move forward, carry the lessons, the laughs, and the victories with you. They're not just memories; they're the building blocks of your ever-evolving story of resilience and achievement. Here's to moving forward, reaching back only to pull others up, and always, always celebrating the journey. Let's keep the fire burning, the goals big, and the celebrations frequent. Onward and upward, champion!

MOD: Celebrate your 30-day challenge success by doing something fun!

Now — do you feel a little lost? Do you wonder what to do next? Well, take a break some days and then go back to Day 1 and start all over again. Do you want to hear a secret? You can repeat this 30-day challenge how many times you want, and even for the rest of your life. I have done it since I was 29, and I am 58 years old now.

III

Part 3: Beyond the Finish Line – Sustaining Your Success

Chapter 4: Maintaining Your Unstoppable Mindset

Hey there, champion! You've hustled through the initial 30 days, sharpening your mental game into what might seem like peak form. But let's switch up the perspective a bit—think of this not as a finish line but as a springboard into the vast ocean of your potential. The real deal is the continuous journey, the day-in and day-out grind that separates the momentary victors from the legendary heroes. This chapter? It's your guide to staying sharp, curious, and ever-evolving, no matter how many trophies or accolades start piling up.

4.1 Continuing the Journey: Lifelong Learning

Commitment to Growth: More Than Just a Game Plan

First off, let's get something straight: learning never stops. Not after a win, not after 30 days, not ever. Adopting a mindset of lifelong learning is like signing up for an endless championship season, where every day offers a new chance to better your best. This approach keeps you agile, not just physically but mentally, allowing you to adapt and thrive no matter what new challenges or opportunities the whistle blows in.

It's easy to fall into the trap of complacency, especially after hitting a big goal or mastering a new skill. But remember, staying the same in a world that's constantly evolving is akin to moving backward. To keep your edge, you've got to keep sharpening it. Embrace the mindset that every practice, every game, every interaction is a chance to learn something new. This doesn't mean turning every second of your life into a nail-biting drill; rather, it's about keeping your eyes and ears open and your mind ready to absorb and adapt.

Staying Informed: Your Info Ammo

Keeping up-to-date with the latest in sports psychology, training techniques, and motivational strategies is like stocking your arsenal with the best weaponry. Subscribe to relevant magazines, blogs, and podcasts that resonate with your sport and your growth path. These resources can be a goldmine of innovative ideas and fresh perspectives that keep you inspired and informed.

For instance, tuning into podcasts such as 'The Hidden Athlete' or reading up on recent articles in 'Sports Psychology Today' can provide insights into mental training techniques you might not have encountered yet. Make it a habit to spend a little time each week exploring new content; think of it as feeding your brain the good stuff, the stuff that keeps it keen and competitive.

Seeking Feedback: The Game Changer

Feedback is the breakfast of champions — without it, growth is stunted. Regularly seek feedback from coaches, peers, and mentors. This isn't about fishing for compliments or stewing in criticism; it's about gaining perspectives that can catalyze your growth. Constructive feedback can shine a light on blind spots and open up new paths to mastery. It's about fine-tuning your skills, adjusting your game plan, and sometimes, just getting the reassurance that you're on the right track.

Make it a two-way street by asking specific questions. Instead of a generic "How did I do?" try "What can I do to improve my swing?" or "Can you suggest a way to enhance my concentration during long matches?" This not only shows your commitment to improvement but also helps you gather targeted and actionable insights.

Professional Development: Never Stop Learning

Investing in your development is investing in your future. Look out for workshops, seminars, and online courses that can help elevate your game. Many sports organizations and training camps offer sessions on everything from nutrition and physical conditioning to mental resilience and leadership. Participating in these can boost your performance and expand your network, connecting you with others who are just as driven to excel.

Consider certifications in areas that interest you, such as a course in sports psychology or a workshop on advanced team dynamics. These enhance your understanding and add to your credentials, opening up new opportunities within and beyond your current sporting endeavors.

Remember, maintaining an unstoppable mindset isn't just about pushing through another set of drills; it's about continuously evolving, learning from each step, and staying open to new possibilities. Your mindset is your most powerful tool — keep it sharp, and it will carve paths to victories you've yet to imagine. So, keep pushing, stay curious, and let every day be a new opportunity to expand your horizons.

4.2 Staying Motivated: Tips and Tricks

Setting New Goals: Your Roadmap to Continuous Improvement

Think of goal-setting as your personal GPS system — it doesn't just guide you to your destination; it keeps you on track and adjusts your route as necessary. That's why continuously setting and revising your goals is crucial. It keeps you engaged, challenges you, and pushes you out of your comfort zone, ensuring that you're not just running in circles but actually sprinting towards something bigger and better.

Start by integrating both MODs, short-term and long-term goals into your routine. Short-term goals are your mile markers — they give you immediate targets to aim for and help build momentum. These could be as simple as improving your time by a few seconds in the next race or mastering a new technique by the end of the month. Long-term goals, on the other hand, are like your final destination. They are the big dreams, such as winning a championship or earning a scholarship. These goals aren't just about keeping you driven; they're about giving your training a purpose and a direction.

But here's the kicker: goals need to be flexible. Life throws curveballs, and your ability to adapt your goals accordingly is what keeps you resilient and motivated. Regularly review your goals, assess your progress, and adjust them if necessary. Maybe you've outpaced your original expectations and need a new challenge, or perhaps you've encountered setbacks and need to recalibrate. This ongoing process of evaluation and adjustment keeps your journey exciting and personally relevant.

What is your Mindset Of the Day (MOD)?

Yes, I have come up with this new abbreviation. Remember in the future where this new term came from when you hear it next time in connection with sports psychology... :-) seriously now — continue to set MODs! Use them to, in small steps, reach your long-term Goals. It doesn't matter if you put them up in the morning the same day or set them for a whole week ahead or just the day before — use them! They literally are the minds equivalent to the physical Workout Of the Day (WODs) used in the CrossFit world to make you stronger and better.

Variety in Training: Keeping It Fresh and Fun

Let's face it, doing the same drills over and over can be as dull as watching paint dry. To keep your training engaging and prevent the dreaded burnout, sprinkle a little variety into your routine. Mixing things up keeps your training fun and challenges different muscles and skills, enhancing your overall athleticism.

Consider cross-training to give your usual routine a twist. If you're a runner, throw in some cycling or swimming. These activities can improve your aerobic capacity while giving your running muscles a break. Or how about incorporating Yoga or Pilates? These can enhance your flexibility and core strength, which are beneficial no matter what your main sport is. Trying out new sports not only breaks the monotony but can also reignite your love for training by introducing new challenges and excitement.

Changing up your workout environment can also refresh your motivation. If you're used to a gym, take your workout to a park or a local track. A change of scenery can invigorate your senses and inject some new energy into your routine. Even altering the time of day you train can make a difference. Usually an evening trainer? Challenge yourself, get out of the comfort zone and try hitting the track early in the morning and let the fresh, crisp air wake up your body and mind.

Maintaining a Positive Environment: Your Motivational Eco-System

Your environment plays a massive role in keeping you motivated. Surrounding yourself with positivity can propel you forward, while a negative atmosphere can drag you down. This goes beyond physical spaces — think about the people around you as well.

Cultivate a support system of friends, family, and teammates who understand your goals and support your efforts. This network can provide encouragement, share in your victories, and help you navigate setbacks. Positive reinforcement from this group can be a powerful motivator, pushing you to keep going when things get tough.

Also, consider your digital environment. Follow athletes and influencers who inspire you and share insights that resonate with your goals. Social media can be a double-edged sword — it can drown you in negativity, or it can be a source of inspiration. Choose wisely whom you let into your virtual space and mind.

Celebrating Small Wins: Every Step Forward Counts

In the grind towards big goals, don't forget to celebrate the small victories. These moments, no matter how minor they seem, are the building blocks of your larger success. They reinforce your belief in your ability to achieve and provide tangible proof that you are moving forward.

Set up a system to acknowledge these achievements. Maybe you jot them down in a journal or share them with a friend or coach. Celebrating these wins doesn't just boost your morale; it also increases your motivation to push towards the next goal. It's about recognizing your progress, which is essential for maintaining a positive and motivated mindset.

Mindfulness and Self-Care: Essential Tools for Your Arsenal

Finally, never underestimate the power of mindfulness and self-care in maintaining your motivation. These practices help you manage stress, focus on the present, and maintain a balanced perspective, which is crucial for long-term motivation.

Incorporate mindfulness exercises into your daily routine. This could be as simple as spending a few minutes each day in meditation or practicing deep-

CHAPTER 4: MAINTAINING YOUR UNSTOPPABLE MINDSET

breathing exercises before a game. These practices help center your mind, giving you clarity and peace — a contrast to the chaotic nature of training and competition.

Self-care is equally important. This includes getting adequate sleep, eating well, and taking time to do things you enjoy outside your sport. Remember, you're not a machine. Taking care of your mental and physical health is crucial, not just for your athletic performance but for your overall well-being.

By focusing on these areas — setting dynamic goals, injecting variety into your training, fostering a positive environment, celebrating small victories, and practicing mindfulness and self-care — you can maintain a high level of motivation that propels you toward your goals. Keep these strategies in mind as you move forward, and remember that motivation, like your muscles, needs both work and rest to grow stronger.

Keeping the Game Alive

Now that you have everything you need to reach greatness, it's time to pass on your newfound knowledge and show other readers where they can find the same help.

Your review could be the beacon that guides them to success, just as this book has been for you.

Simply scan the QR code above to leave your review:

If you feel good about helping someone else, you're the person we need in our community. Welcome to the club. You're one of us.

Thank you for your support and for helping keep the game alive. I'm thrilled to see how you will confidently apply the knowledge in this book to adventure safely.

If you e-mail a link to your posted review here: review-support@stoneport.se I will send you a 30-Day Journal Template in PDF format to print out and use together with this book to simplify your journaling!

- Your biggest fan, Mixon Stenhamn

PS - Sharing is caring! If you found value in this book, consider passing it on to someone who might benefit. Let's keep the cycle of knowledge and support going strong.

Chapter 5: Applying Your Skills Beyond Sports

Hey there, champ! You've been flexing those mental muscles on the field, mastering the art of mental toughness, focus, and resilience. But what if I told you that the skills you've been honing aren't just for scoring goals or acing matches? That's right, the discipline of a dedicated athlete can turn you into a superstar off the field too. From acing your academics to climbing the career ladder and even being a rock star in your personal relationships, the skills you've developed in sports can give you a competitive edge in pretty much every arena of life. So, let's explore how you can take your game-day mindset and make it work overtime, transforming every aspect of your daily life.

5.1 Transferring Your Mindset to Other Areas of Life

Academic Success

Let's kick off with your academics. Think about it; sports require discipline, focus, and the ability to set and achieve goals — sounds a lot like what you need to excel in school, right? Here's the game plan: Treat your study sessions like practice sessions. Set specific goals for each study period, just like you would for training. Maybe it's mastering a certain number of algebra problems or understanding a scientific concept.

CHAPTER 5: APPLYING YOUR SKILLS BEYOND SPORTS

Just like in sports, resilience in your academic endeavors means seeing a bad grade as a chance to improve, not as a failure. It's about asking for feedback, hitting the books, and coming back stronger, not unlike reviewing game tape and working on weak spots before the next match. Remember, every athlete knows the pain of defeat, but it's bouncing back that makes you better.

Career Development

Now, let's talk career. Whether you dream of being a corporate leader, a tech guru, or the next entrepreneurial sensation, the qualities that make you a great athlete can also make you a standout in the workplace. Goal setting is your bread and butter, right? Apply that to your career ambitions. Set short-term and long-term career goals, identify the skills you need to develop and create a roadmap to get there.

Handling pressure is another area where athletes excel. In your career, this translates to managing deadlines, dealing with tough clients, or handling high-stakes negotiations. Your ability to stay calm under pressure, a skill you've refined in countless down-to-the-wire games, can set you apart in any high-stress professional environment.

Personal Relationships

Switching gears to personal relationships — here, communication, teamwork, and empathy come into play. These are the same skills that make you a great team player. In relationships, it's about listening, understanding different perspectives, and working together towards common goals. Whether it's with a partner, friends, or family, showing that you can be a team player helps in building stronger, more supportive relationships.

And let's not forget empathy. On the field, you quickly learn that every team member has their strengths and struggles. This understanding can make you a more compassionate friend, partner, or family member, someone who recognizes others' challenges and offers support just like a true teammate would.

Community Involvement

Lastly, your role in the community. Athletes are often seen as role models, and for a good reason. You have the power to inspire and influence those around you. Consider volunteering, mentoring young athletes, or organizing community sports events. Your involvement can energize and uplift your community, and the leadership skills you develop in the process are invaluable.

Plus, engaging with your community isn't just about giving back. It's also about growing your network, understanding diverse perspectives, and building a support system that extends beyond the field. It's a win-win. You inspire others, and every interaction and every shared experience enriches your own life.

So there you have it: transferring your sports mindset to your life outside of athletics isn't just possible; it's a strategic move that can help you score big across the board. Whether it's acing that exam, climbing the career ladder, or nurturing relationships, the discipline, focus, and resilience you've cultivated as an athlete are the very skills that can lead you to success. Keep playing the long game, and watch as the world becomes your field.

5.2 Success Stories: From Athletes to Leaders

So, you've been hitting the ground running, throwing punches, and scoring goals, but ever wonder what happens when athletes hang up their jerseys? Some of the most inspiring tales come from those who've transitioned from the sports arena to leading roles in various fields. These stories aren't just about switching careers; they're about transferring a mindset honed in sports to conquer completely different worlds.

Take, for instance, the legendary Magic Johnson. After an illustrious NBA career, he didn't just retire to a life of leisure; he turned his leadership on the court into leadership in the business and philanthropic worlds. Magic saw opportunities, whereas others saw obstacles. His venture into business started with movie theaters in underserved neighborhoods, then expanded into a business empire that includes everything from gyms to Starbucks franchises, all while championing urban development and HIV/AIDS awareness. His success stems from his incredible vision, tenacity, and the ability to inspire and rally people around him — qualities every great athlete needs.

Then there's the phenomenal Bill Bradley, a former NBA player who pivoted to a distinguished political career. Bradley took the teamwork, discipline, and strategic planning he learned on the basketball court to the U.S. Senate. He focused on complex issues like tax reform and health care, applying the same dedication and work ethic that made him a sports star to serve his country at a high level. His career is a powerful reminder that the qualities that make you a great athlete can also make you a great leader in any field.

Lessons from Leaders

Diving deeper, let's extract some universal lessons from these crossover champions. A common theme among them is the ability to set clear, ambitious goals. Just as they set sports goals, they set life and career goals with the same intensity and clarity. They also maintain an incredible work ethic, often outworking their peers in whatever new fields they choose to conquer.

Resilience, a trait all athletes develop, also plays a crucial role. The setbacks in sports — losing games, injuries, bad seasons — are mirrored in life and business challenges. Yet, these leaders use resilience to fuel their rise, not deter it. They adapt, learn, and push forward, using failures as stepping stones, not stop signs.

Another key trait is the ability to inspire and lead a team. Leadership in sports translates effectively into leadership in business or any other arena because it's all about motivating people toward a common goal, recognizing their strengths, and helping them overcome weaknesses. Effective communication, another skill refined in sports, ensures these leaders are both heard and understood, rallying their teams to victory in boardrooms or community projects.

Your Own Leadership Journey

Now, think about how you can apply these insights to your own potential as a leader. Start by envisioning where you want to make an impact. Is it in business, education, community service, or perhaps politics? Reflect on the skills and experiences you've gained through sports that can translate into effective leadership in these areas.

Begin by setting small, achievable goals that align with your larger vision. For example, if you're interested in community service, start by volunteering in local initiatives. If business is your field of interest, consider internships or joining related clubs and societies that can provide both experience and networking opportunities.

Developing leadership skills also involves continually seeking feedback and being open to learning—traits you're already practicing in sports. Engage with mentors, attend workshops, and read extensively. Leaders are often voracious learners, always looking to broaden their knowledge and improve their skills.

Lastly, never underestimate the power of your example. Just as younger athletes might look up to you on the field, others will follow your lead in other areas of life. Embrace this role with responsibility and enthusiasm. Lead by example, be generous with your time and knowledge, and always strive to uplift others along your path.

CHAPTER 5: APPLYING YOUR SKILLS BEYOND SPORTS

As you continue to navigate the vast opportunities beyond the sports arenas, remember that the qualities that brought you success in athletics—discipline, resilience, goal orientation, teamwork, and leadership—are the very ones that will define your success in any field. Keep honing these skills, stay curious, and keep challenging yourself. The world is wide, and your potential is limitless.

Transitioning into the next chapter, we'll explore how to sustain and grow these leadership qualities, ensuring they define your success and contribute positively to the communities and fields you choose to influence. Let's keep pushing the boundaries, expanding our horizons, and setting new benchmarks in every walk of life.

Conclusion: Your New Beginning

Alright, team, we've sprinted through the mental marathon together, from diving headfirst into the deep waters of mental toughness to scaling the dizzy heights of maintaining an unstoppable mindset. You've laced up your boots, strapped on your armor, and shown up every single day, ready to tackle whatever drills I threw your way. Now, as we cool down and stretch out those well-worked mental muscles, let's take a moment to reflect on our journey and gear up for what's next.

Remember back in Chapter 1 when we talked about the power of mindset? That wasn't just a pep talk. Embracing a growth mindset isn't about wearing rose-tinted glasses; it's about seeing each challenge as a stepping stone, not a stumbling block. You've learned that setbacks aren't stop signs — they're just signposts pointing toward improvement.

We ventured through the landscapes of confidence, focus, and resilience, equipping you with the tools not just to survive but to thrive under pressure, in sports and beyond. Each strategy and story was chosen to help you build a mental toolkit that's as robust as a well-packed survival kit. Why? Because whether you're facing a grueling tournament or a tough exam, the right mindset can make you or break you.

Now, why did I, Mixon, martial arts coach, wilderness survival assistant, and business consultant, take you on this journey? Because I believe in the power of transformation. I've seen it on the mats, in the wilderness, and in the boardroom. Mental toughness isn't just about pushing through; it's about pivoting, adapting, and coming out stronger on the other side. It's about not just meeting life's challenges but greeting them, with your head held high and your spirits even higher.

As we wrap up, I urge you not just to read, but to act. Take these lessons, try out the exercises, fill your daily journals, and most importantly, keep pushing your limits. Set new goals, no matter how lofty; explore new challenges, no matter how daunting. And remember, the real competition isn't with others — it's with the person you were yesterday. Aim to be a better version of that person; Every. Single. Day.

And as you step out into your world, whether it's the track, the field, the classroom, or the office, carry with you the essence of what we've shared. Let it not just be knowledge, but action; not just memory, but habit. Your journey to mental toughness doesn't end here — it's just getting started.

So, here's your final call to action: Go out there and be unstoppable. Not because it's easy, but because you're ready. Ready to tackle the hard stuff, ready to face the unknown, and ready to transform challenges into triumphs.

Thank you for allowing me to be part of your journey to greatness. Remember, the path to success is always under construction. Keep building, keep growing, and most importantly, keep moving forward. Let's set the world on fire with our unbreakable spirit and unwavering resolve. Here's to your continued success, both in sports and in life!

Reflecting on the 30-Day Challenge

- **Celebrating Achievements**: Take a moment to acknowledge the hard work and dedication you've put into this 30-day journey. Reflect on the progress you've made, the challenges you've overcome, and the skills you've developed.
- **Key Takeaways**: Summarize the main lessons and strategies you've learned throughout the book. Consider how these lessons have impacted

your mindset, performance, and overall well-being.
- **Personal Growth**: Reflect on your personal growth during the past month. How have your confidence, focus, and resilience improved? What new habits have you formed? How has your approach to challenges and setbacks changed?

Encouragement for the Future

- **Embracing Continuous Improvement**: Encourage yourself to continue striving for improvement. Remember that growth is a lifelong journey, and there are always new goals to achieve and new skills to develop.
- **Setting New Goals**: Use the momentum from the past 30 days to set new, ambitious goals. Whether in sports, academics, career, or personal life, keep challenging yourself to reach new heights.
- **Staying Motivated**: Find ways to maintain your motivation. Remind yourself of why you started this journey and the benefits you've experienced. Stay connected to your support system and continue celebrating your progress.

Stay Unstoppable: Final Words of Wisdom

- **Believe in Yourself**: Always remember that the key to an unstoppable mindset lies within you. Trust in your abilities, stay confident, and never doubt your potential to achieve greatness.
- **Embrace Challenges**: View challenges as opportunities for growth. Each setback is a chance to learn and improve. Stay resilient and keep pushing forward, no matter the obstacles.
- **Step out of the Comfort zone Regurlarly:** Always challenge yourself. Comfort kills you slowly. It is when you are uncomfortable you thrive and grow.
- **Practice Gratitude**: Cultivate an attitude of gratitude. Appreciate your journey, the people who support you, and the progress you make. Gratitude will keep you grounded and positive.

- **Stay Balanced**: Maintain a healthy balance in your life. Ensure you're giving attention to all aspects of your well-being, including physical, mental, emotional, and social health. Balance will help you sustain your progress and enjoy the journey.
- **Inspire Others**: Use your journey to inspire and support others. Share your experiences, mentor younger athletes, and contribute to your community. Your positive influence can make a significant impact on those around you.

By reflecting on your accomplishments and embracing the lessons learned during the 30-day challenge, you are well-equipped to continue your journey with an unstoppable mindset. Remember, this is just the beginning. Stay committed to your growth, remain resilient in the face of challenges, and keep striving for excellence in all areas of your life. Your potential is limitless — stay unstoppable!

The secret essence of mental toughness and the 7 essential components that contribute to a resilient mindset

A resilient mindset is essential for overcoming challenges and maintaining mental toughness. Here are 7 essential components that contribute to a resilient mindset:

1. Positive Thinking

- **Definition:** Cultivating an optimistic outlook and focusing on the good in any situation.
- **Impact:** Helps maintain motivation, reduce stress, and improve overall mental health.

2. Emotional Regulation

- **Definition:** The ability to manage and respond to emotional experiences healthily.
- **Impact:** Prevents emotional overload and promotes a balanced approach to dealing with stress and adversity.

3. Self-Efficacy

- **Definition:** Belief in one's ability to influence events and outcomes in one's own life.
- **Impact:** Encourages proactive behavior, persistence, and confidence to tackle challenges.

4. Adaptability

- **Definition:** The capacity to adjust to new conditions and embrace change.
- **Impact:** Enhances the ability to thrive in dynamic environments and reduces anxiety associated with the unknown.

5. Strong Social Support

- **Definition:** Having a network of family, friends, and mentors to rely on.
- **Impact:** Provides emotional support, practical help, and a sense of belonging, which are crucial during tough times.

6. Goal Setting

- **Definition:** Identifying and committing to specific, measurable, achievable, relevant, and time-bound (SMART) objectives.
- **Impact:** Focuses efforts, enhances motivation, and provides a sense of purpose and direction.

7. Problem-Solving Skills

- **Definition:** The ability to identify, analyze, and solve problems effectively.
- **Impact:** Reduces feelings of helplessness, promotes resourcefulness, and encourages a proactive approach to overcoming obstacles.

By integrating these components, individuals can develop a resilient mindset that empowers them to face challenges head-on and emerge stronger.

The 5 proven strategies for setting practical performance goals and achieving them:

Setting practical performance goals and achieving them requires a strategic approach. Here are 5 proven strategies:

1. Define SMART Goals

- **Specific:** Clearly define what you want to achieve.
- **Measurable:** Establish criteria to track progress and measure success.
- **Achievable:** Set realistic and attainable goals.
- **Relevant:** Ensure the goals align with your broader objectives.
- **Time-bound:** Set a deadline for achieving the goals.
- **Impact:** Provides clarity, focus, and a framework for assessing progress.

2. Break Down Goals into Smaller Steps

- **Strategy:** Divide larger goals into smaller, manageable tasks or milestones.
- **Impact:** Reduces overwhelm, maintains motivation, and makes the process more manageable.

3. Create an Action Plan

- **Strategy:** Develop a detailed plan outlining the steps, resources, and

timeline needed to achieve each goal.
- **Impact:** Provides a clear roadmap, keeps you organized, and helps you stay on track.

4. Regular Monitoring and Adjustment

- **Strategy:** Frequently review your progress and make necessary adjustments.
- **Impact:** It ensures you remain on course, allows for flexibility in responding to challenges, and keeps the goals relevant.

5. Leverage Accountability and Support

- **Strategy:** Share your goals with others and seek feedback, support, and accountability from mentors, coaches, or peers.
- **Impact:** Enhances commitment, provides motivation, and offers guidance and support during challenging times.

By applying these strategies, individuals can set practical performance goals and create a structured path to achieving them, increasing the likelihood of success.

Appendices

With these resources, journaling pages, and support information, you will have the tools to continue your journey towards an unstoppable mindset, ensuring sustained success and personal growth in all areas of your life.

Resources for Further Reading

Books:

"Mindset: The New Psychology of Success" by Carol S. Dweck
   Description: This book explores the concept of fixed and growth mindsets and how these mindsets impact success in various areas of life, including sports, business, and education.

"The Champion's Mind: How Great Athletes Think, Train, and Thrive" by Jim Afremow
   Description: Offers insights into the mental strategies used by elite athletes, covering topics such as focus, resilience, and the importance of mental preparation.

"Grit: The Power of Passion and Perseverance" by Angela Duckworth
   Description: Discusses the importance of grit, which combines passion and perseverance, in achieving long-term goals. Duckworth presents research and real-life examples of how grit can lead to success.

"Relentless: From Good to Great to Unstoppable" by Tim S. Grover
   Description: Provides a look into the mindset of top athletes and the principles that drive them to be relentless in their pursuit of greatness.

Articles and Journals:

"The Role of Sports Psychology in Athletic Success"
   Source: Journal of Sports Science and Medicine
   Description: Explores how sports psychology interventions can enhance athletic performance and well-being.
   Link: Journal of Sports Science and Medicine

"Mental Toughness and Athletic Performance"
   Source: International Journal of Sport and Exercise Psychology
   Description: Examines the relationship between mental toughness and various aspects of athletic performance.

Websites and Blogs:

Psychology Today: Sports Psychology Section
   Description: Provides articles and insights from experts in sports psychology on various topics related to mental training and performance.

Athlete Assessments
   Description: Offers resources and tools for athletes and coaches to assess and improve mental performance.
   Link: Athlete Assessments

The Mindful Athlete
   Description: Features articles and resources focused on mindfulness and mental training for athletes.
   Link: The Mindful Athlete

Podcasts and Videos:

"The Tim Ferriss Show"
Description: Features interviews with high-performing athletes and coaches, discussing their mental strategies and routines.

"Finding Mastery" with Michael Gervais
Description: Explores the psychology behind success in sports through interviews with top athletes, coaches, and psychologists.
Link: Finding Mastery

"The MindSide Podcast"
Description: Discusses mental training and sports psychology with experts and athletes, offering practical tips and insights.

By incorporating insights and techniques from these resources, you can develop a resilient and unstoppable mindset that supports your journey to peak performance.

RESOURCES FOR FURTHER READING

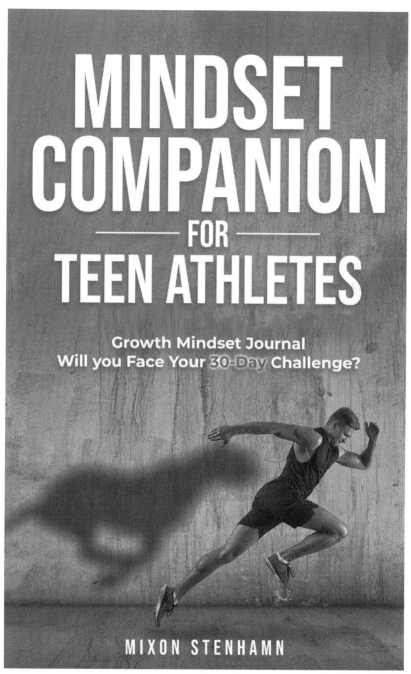

This is the Companion Journal to this Book you can find on Amazon to facilitate your journaling through your 30-Day Challenge.

This is the Parents Book you can find on Amazon to support you through your 30-Day Challenge fully and beyond.

Journaling Page for Daily, Weekly & Monthly Reflections

You can find a journaling template here if you are not using my "Mindset Companion for Teen Athletes: Growth Mindset Journal — Will you Face Your 30-Day Challenge?".

Daily Reflection Template: This is a template for daily reflection, including sections for goal setting, achievements, challenges, and lessons learned. Use these questions to track your progress and stay focused on your journey.

- **Date:**
- **Today's Goal:** What is the primary objective you want to accomplish today?
- **Achievements:** What did you achieve today, no matter how small?
- **Challenges:** What obstacles did you encounter today?
- **Lessons Learned:** What did you learn from today's experiences?
- **Gratitude Reflection:** What are you grateful for today?
- **Tomorrow's Goal:** What is your primary objective for tomorrow?

Weekly Reflection Prompts: Prompts for weekly reflection to help you assess your progress, celebrate successes, and plan for the upcoming week.

- What were my biggest achievements this week?
- What challenges did I face, and how did I overcome them?
- What lessons have I learned this week?
- What am I grateful for this week?

- What are my goals for next week?

Monthly Reflection and Goal Setting: to help you review your long-term progress and set new goals.

Reflecting on the Past Month:

- What were my most significant achievements this month?
- What challenges did I face, and how did I overcome them?
- What lessons have I learned this month?
- What am I grateful for this month?

Setting Goals for the Next Month:

- What are my top three goals for the next month?
- What steps will I take to achieve these goals?
- How will I stay motivated and accountable?

How to Use this Journaling Page:

1. **Consistency:** Make journaling a daily habit. Spend a few minutes each day reflecting and writing down your thoughts.
2. **Honesty:** Be truthful with yourself in your reflections. Acknowledge both your strengths and areas for improvement.
3. **Focus:** Use your goals to guide your actions and stay focused on your journey.
4. **Celebrate:** Recognize and celebrate your achievements, no matter how small.
5. **Growth:** Use the challenges and lessons learned as opportunities for growth and improvement.

Support and Community Resources for Athletes

By leveraging these resources, you can build a strong support network, access professional guidance, and utilize tools that enhance your mental and physical performance.

Online Communities

Connecting with peers and experts through online communities can provide invaluable support and advice. Here are some recommended forums and social media groups:

Reddit: r/sportspsychology: A community for discussions on sports psychology, mental training, and performance enhancement.

Facebook Groups

Sports Psychology Network: A group for athletes, coaches, and sports psychology professionals to share insights and support.

Athlete Mental Training Support: A supportive community focused on mental training and resilience for athletes.

Online Forums

Let's Run: A forum for runners and athletes to discuss training, races, and mental strategies.

The Sports Psychologist's Community
   Visit Sports Psychologists Directory and find community discussions and resources.

Local Organizations and Clubs

Joining local sports clubs and organizations can provide in-person support and a sense of community. Here's how athletes can find these groups in their area:

Local Sports Clubs and Leagues:

How to Find: Search online for local sports clubs or leagues in your city or town, check community bulletin boards, or ask for recommendations at local gyms.

Community Centers Offering Sports Programs:

How to Find: Visit your local community center or its website to see what sports programs and classes are available.

University and School Sports Teams and Clubs:

How to Find: Check with your school's athletic department or website for information on sports teams and clubs you can join.

Professional Support

Accessing professional support can provide personalized guidance and expertise. Here are some resources for finding sports psychologists, coaches, and mentors:

National and Regional Associations of Sports Psychologists:

Association for Applied Sport Psychology (AASP): AASP Directory
American Psychological Association (APA) - Division 47 (Exercise and Sport Psychology): APA Division 47

Directory of Certified Mental Performance Consultants:

CMPC Directory: Find certified mental performance consultants through the AASP directory.

Local Coaches and Training Centers:

How to Find: Search for local sports coaches and training centers online, or ask for recommendations from your local sports club or gym.

Additional Resources

Utilize apps, tools, and workshops to maintain progress and continue developing an unstoppable mindset:

Meditation and Mindfulness Apps:

Headspace

Calm

Goal-Setting and Productivity Apps:

Trello

Asana

Upcoming Workshops and Seminars:

Check local event listings, university sports programs, and websites like Eventbrite for workshops and seminars on sports psychology and athlete development.

About the Author

As a multifaceted professional and seasoned martial arts instructor and Coach, Mixon has dedicated his life to empowering individuals through the disciplined practice of martial arts, including Yoga, Fitness, Crosstraining, HIIT, and Outdoor Boot Camp. His passion for physical fitness and mental toughness training is evident in every class he leads, where he inspires his students to push beyond their limits and achieve their personal bests.

In addition to his martial arts expertise, Mixon was trained in outdoor survival when serving in the Swedish Military as Commander of a Reconnaissance Platoon, as a Scout leader, and later at All In Nature Sweden (AINS). He now works as an assistant instructor at AINS in outdoor safety, first aid, and survival. His mission is to ensure that every individual—whether a child embarking on their first hike, a teenager eager to explore, or a family planning a camping trip—can do so with the assurance and joy of being prepared.

You can connect with me on:
- https://books.stoneport.se
- https://x.com/MixonsS
- https://www.facebook.com/Mixon.PT
- https://www.youtube.com/@mixonsstoneport8708/videos